The Lord Will Fight For You

By Diana Akagi

THE LORD WILL FIGHT FOR YOU

Preface..

The Purpose of this Book is to bring comfort to those who have lived with fear all their life.

They can be sure that, you can live with peace of mind and a worry free life through Christ Jesus.

Scripture Arranged By
Diana Akagi

Design & Typesetting
by
Michael Rudd

Printed By
Graphic Creative
Marina del Rey, California

1.310.928.3989
Mailbox@GraphicCreative.com
Graphic Creative

Scriptures Taken From

The New King James Version ®
Copyright © 1982 by Thomas Nelson Inc.
Thomas Nelson Publishers
Nashville • Atlanta • London • Vancouver

Permission by Mardi West

(615) 902-1521

THE LORD WILL FIGHT FOR YOU

Table of Contents

THE LORD WILL FIGHT FOR YOU

The Lord Will

Fight For You

THE LORD WILL FIGHT FOR YOU

The Lord Will Fight For You

✧

GENESIS 6:3

And the Lord said, "My Spirit shall not strive with man forever, for he is indeed flesh; yet his days shall be one hundred and twenty years."

✧

EXODUS 14:14

"The Lord will fight for you, and you shall hold your peace."

✧

DEUTERONOMY 1:30

The Lord your God, who goes before you, He will fight for you, according to all He did for you in Egypt before your eyes,

✧

DEUTERONOMY 3:22

'You must not fear them, for the Lord your God Himself fights for you.'

✧

PSALM 118:6

The Lord is on my side; I will not fear. What can man do to me?

✧

PSALM 138:7

Though I walk in the midst of trouble, You will revive me; You will stretch out Your hand Against the wrath of my enemies, And Your right hand will save me.

✧

JEREMIAH 15:21

"I will deliver you from the hand of the wicked, And I will redeem you from the grip of the terrible."

✧

DEUTERONOMY 31:6

"Be strong and of good courage, do not fear nor be afraid of them; for the Lord your God, He is the One who goes with you. He will not leave you nor forsake you."

Merciful God

✧

EXODUS 15:26

and said, "If you diligently heed the voice of the Lord your God and do what is right in His sight, give ear to His commandments and keep all His statutes, I will put none of the diseases on you which I have brought on the Egyptians. For I am the Lord who heals you."

✧

EXODUS 23:22

"But if you indeed obey His voice and do all that I speak, then I will be an enemy to your enemies and an adversary to your adversaries.

✧

DEUTERONOMY 31:8

"And the Lord, He is the One who goes before you. He will be with you, He will not leave you nor forsake you; do not fear nor be dismayed."

✧

PSALM 11:7

For the Lord is righteous, He loves righteousness; His countenance beholds the upright.

✧

PSALM 18:32

It is God who arms me with strength, And makes my way perfect.

✧

PSALM 100:5

For the Lord is good; His mercy is everlasting, And His truth endures to all generations.

✧

PSALM 103:8

The Lord is merciful and gracious, Slow to anger, and abounding in mercy.

✧

PSALM 103:17

But the mercy of the Lord is from everlasting to everlasting, On those who fear Him, And His righteousness to children's children,

✧

PSALM 142:2

I pour out my complaint before Him; I declare before Him my trouble.

✧

ISAIAH 45:2

'I will go before you And make the crooked places straight; I will break in pieces the gates of bronze And cut the bars of iron.

✧

DEUTERONOMY 4:31

"(for the Lord your God is a merciful God), He will not forsake you nor destroy you, nor forget the covenant of your fathes which He swore to them.

✧

PSALM 145:8

The Lord is gracious and full of compassion, Slow to anger and great in mercy.

✧

PSALM 145:9

The Lord is good to all, And His tender mercies are over all His works.

✧

PSALM 145:13

Your kingdom is an everlasting kingdom, And Your dominion endures throughout all generations.

✧

PSALM 45:17

I will make Your name to be remembered in all generations; Therefore the people shall praise You forever and ever.

✧

PSALM 145:19

He will fulfill the desire of those who fear Him; He also will hear their cry and save them.

✧

PSALM 147:6

The Lord lifts up the humble; He casts the wicked down to the ground.

✧

ISAIAH 66:13

As one whom his mother comforts, So I will comfort you; And you shall be comforted in Jerusalem."

✧

MICAH 7:19

He will again have compassion on us, And will subdue our iniquities. You will cast all our sins Into the depths of the sea.

✧

NAHUM 1:3

The Lord is slow to anger and great in power, And will not at all acquit the wicked. The Lord has His way In the whirlwind and in the storm, And the clouds are the dust of His feet.

✧

NAHUM 1:7

The Lord is good, A stronghold in the day of trouble; and He knows those who trust in Him.

✧

ROMANS 11:30

For as you were once disobedient to God, yet have now obtained mercy through their disobedience,

✧

✧

HEBREWS 2:9

But we see Jesus, who was made a little lower than the angels, for the suffering of death crowned with glory and honor, that He, by the grace of God, might taste death for everyone.

✧

HEBREWS 4:15

For we do not have a High Priest who cannot sympathize with our weaknesses, but was in all points tempted as we are, yet without sin.

✧

II. PETER 3:9

The Lord is not slack concerning His promise, as some count slackness, but is longsuffering toward us, not willing that any should perish but that all should come to repentance.

✧

I. JOHN 1:9

If we confess our sins, He is faithful and just to forgive us our sins and cleanse us from all unrighteousness.

✧

JUDE 1:21

Keep yourselves in the love of God, looking for the mercy of our Lord Jesus Christ unto eternal life.

✧

PSALM 57:11

Be exalted, O God, above the heavens; Let Your glory be above all the earth.

✧

PSALM 59:1

Deliver me from my enemies, O my God; Defend me from those who rise up against me.

✧

PSALM 108:4

For Your mercy is great above the heavens, And your truth reaches
to the clouds.

PSALM 116:5

Gracious is the Lord, and righteous; Yes, our God is merciful. The Lord
preserves the simple; I was brought low, and He saved me.

PSALM 116:8

For You have delivered my soul from death, My eyes from tears, And my
feet from falling.

LAMENTATION 3:25

The Lord is good to those who wait for Him, To the soul who seeks Him.

LAMENTATION 3:26

It is good that one should hope and wait quietly For the salvation
of the Lord.

COLOSSIANS 2:14

having wiped out the handwriting of requirements that was against us,
which was contrary to us. And He has taken it out of the way, having nailed
it to the cross.

COLOSSIANS 2:15

Having disarmed principalities and powers, He made a public spectacle of
them, triumphing over them in it.

II THESSALONIANS 3:3

But the Lord is faithful, who will establish you and guard you from
the evil one.

II TIMOTHY 1:7
For God has not given us a spirit of fear, but of power and of love and of a sound mind.

II TIMOTHY 4:18
And the Lord will deliver me from every evil work and preserve me for His heavenly kingdom. To Him be glory forever and ever. Amen!

PSALM 55:22
Cast your burden on the Lord, And He shall sustain you; He shall never permit the righteous to be moved.

PSALM 62:8
Trust in Him at all times, you people; Pour out your heart before Him; God is a refuge for us.

JEREMIAH 33:3
'Call to Me, and I will and answer you, and show you great and mighty things, which you do not know.'

JEREMIAH 39:18
"For I will surely delivery you, and you shall not fall by the sword; but your life shall be as a prize to you, because you have put your trust in Me," says the Lord.'"

JOB 4:4
Your words have upheld him who was stumbling, And you have strengthened the feeble knees;

PSALM 77:15
You have with Your arm redeemed Your people, The sons of Jacob and Joseph.

✧

PSALM 78:39

For He remembered that they were but flesh, A breath that passes away
and does not come again.

✧

DANIEL 6:27

He delivers and rescues, And He works signs and wonders In heaven and
on earth, Who has delivered Daniel from the power of the lions.

✧

PSALM 27:11

Teach me Your way, O Lord, And lead me in a smooth path, because
of my enemies.

✧

PSALM 27:14

Wait on the Lord; Be of good courage, And He shall strengthen your heart;
Wait, I say, on the Lord!

✧

PSALM 118:17

I shall not die, but live, And declare the works of the Lord.

✧

PSALM 119:133

Direct my steps by Your words, And let no iniquity have
dominion over me.

✧

PSALM 119:142

Your righteousness is an everlasting righteousness, And Your law is truth.

✧

PSALM 119:156

Great are Your tender mercies, O Lord; Revive me according
to Your judgments.

✧

✧

PSALM 135:13
Your name, O Lord, endures forever, Your fame, O Lord, throughout all generations.

✧

PSALM 135:14
For the Lord will judge His people, And He will have compassion on His servants.

✧

PSALM 147:3
He heals the brokenhearted And binds up their wounds.

✧

PSALM 147:11
The Lord takes pleasure in those who fear Him, In those who hope in His mercy.

✧

PROVERB 2:6
For the Lord gives wisdom; From His mouth come knowledge and understanding;

✧

PROVERB 2:7
He stores up sound wisdom for the upright; He is a shield to those who walk uprightly;

✧

PROVERB 2:8
He guards the paths of justice, And preserves the way of His saints.

✧

PROVERB 3:13
Happy is the man who finds wisdom, And the man who gains understanding;

✧

PROVERB 5:21

For the ways of man are before the eyes of the Lord, And He ponders all his paths.

ISAIAH 51:12

"I, even I, am He who comforts you. Who are you that you should be afraid Of a man who will die, And of the son of a man who will be made like grass?

ISAIAH 55:8

"For My thoughts are not your thoughts, Nor are your ways My ways," says the Lord.

ISAIAH 55:9

"For as the heavens are higher than the earth, So are My ways higher than your ways, And My thoughts than your thoughts.

JEREMIAH 1:8

Do not be afraid of their faces, For I am with you to deliver you," says the Lord.

DANIEL 4:3

How great are His signs, And how mighty His wonders! His kingdom is an everlasting kingdom, And His dominion is from generation to generation.

I CORINTHIANS 15:4

and that He was buried, and that He rose again the third day according to the Scriptures,

✧

HEBREWS 10:16

"This is the covenant that I will make with them after those days, says the Lord: I will put My laws into their hearts, and in their minds I will write them."

✧

HEBREWS 10:17

then He adds, "Their sins and their lawless deeds I will remember no more."

✧

HEBREWS 10:23

Let us hold fast the confession of our hope without wavering, for He who promised is faithful.

✧

Give Thanks and Praise

✧

EXODUS 23:25

"So you shall serve the Lord your God, and He will bless your bread and your water. And I will take sickness away from the midst of you.

✧

NUMBERS 23:19

God is not a man, that He should lie, Nor a son of man, that He should repent. Has He said, and will He not do? Or has He spoken, and will He not make it good?

✧

NUMBERS 23:26

So Balaam answered and said to Balak, "Did I not tell you, saying, 'All that the Lord speaks, that I must do'?"

✧

PSALM 15:1

Lord, who may abide in Your tabernacle? Who may dwell in Your holy hill?

✧

PSALM 15:2

He who walks uprightly, And works righteousness, And speaks the truth in his heart;

✧

PSALM 15:3

He who does not backbite with his tongue, Nor does evil to his neighbor, Nor does he take up a reproach against his friend;

✧

PSALM 145:2

Every day I will bless You, And I will praise Your name forever and ever.

✧

✧

DEUTERONOMY 7:9

"Therefore know that the Lord your God, He is God, the faithful God who keeps covenant and mercy for a thousand generations with those who love Him and keep His commandments;

✧

DEUTERONOMY 33:27

The eternal God is your refuge, And underneath are the everlasting arms;

✧

JOSHUA 23:6

"Therefore be very courageous to keep and to do all that is written in the Book of the Law of Moses, lest you turn aside from it to the right hand or to the left.

✧

I SAMUEL 12:22

"For the Lord will not forsake His people, for His great name's sake because it has pleased the Lord to make you His people.

✧

I KING 8:23

and he said: "Lord God of Israel, there is no God in heaven above or on earth below like You, who keep Your covenants and mercy with Your servants who walk before You with all their hearts.

✧

PSALM 86:15

But You, O Lord, are a God full of compassion, and gracious, Longsuffering and abundant in mercy and truth.

✧

PSALM 91:1

He who dwells in the secret place of the Most High Shall abide under the shadow of the Almighty.

✧

PSALM 91:2

I will say of the Lord, "He is my refuge and my fortress; My God, in Him I will trust."

✧

✧

ISAIAH 32:18

My people will dwell in a peaceful habitation, In secure dwellings, and in quiet resting places,

✧

ISAIAH 59:1

Behold, the Lord's hand is not shortened, That it cannot save; Nor His ear heavy, That it cannot hear.

✧

LUKE 18:27

But He said, "The things which are impossible with men are possible with God."

✧

JOHN 1:4

In Him was life, and the life was the light of men.

✧

JOHN 1:12

But as many as received Him, to them He gave the right to become children of God, to those who believe in His name:

✧

II CORINTHIANS 1:9

Yes, we had the sentence of death in ourselves, that we should not trust in ourselves but in God who raises the dead,

✧

GALATIANS 1:3

Grace to you and peace from God the Father and our Lord Jesus Christ,

✧

GALATIANS 1:4

who gave Himself for our sins, that He might deliver us from this present evil age, according to the will of our God and Father,

✧

GALATIANS 4:6

And because you are sons, God has sent forth the Spirit of His Son into your hearts, crying out, "Abba, Father!"

✧

◇

EPHESIANS 3:16

that He would grant you, according to the riches of His glory, to be
strengthened with might through His Spirit in the inner man,

◇

EPHESIANS 3:17

that Christ may dwell in your hearts through faith; that you, being rooted
and grounded in love,

◇

I CHRONICLES 16:8

Oh, give thanks to the Lord! Call upon His name; Make known His deeds
among the peoples!

◇

I CHRONICLES 16:9

Sing to Him, sing psalms to Him; Talk of all His wondrous works!

◇

I CHRONICLES 16:14

He is the Lord our God; His judgements are in all the earth.

◇

I CHRONICLES 23:30

to stand every morning to thank and praise the Lord, and likewise at
evening;

◇

II CHRONICLES 6:14

and he said: "Lord God of Israel, there is no God in heaven or on earth
like You, who keep Your covenant and mercy with Your servants who walk
before You with all their hearts.

◇

II CHRONICLES 6:19

"Yet regard the prayer of Your servant and his supplication, O Lord my
God, and listen to the cry and the prayer which Your servant is
praying before You:

◇

II CHRONICLES 6:21

"And may You hear the supplications of Your servant and of Your people Israel, when they pray toward this place. Hear from heaven Your dwelling place, and when You hear, forgive.

✧

PSALM 4:5

Offer the sacrifices of righteousness, And put your trust in the Lord.

✧

PSALM 5:11

But let all those rejoice who put their trust in You; Let them ever shout for joy, because You defend them; Let those also who love Your name Be joyful in You.

✧

PSALM 5:12

For You, O Lord, will bless the righteous, With favor You will surround him as with a shield.

✧

PSALM 7:11

God is a just judge, And God is angry with the wicked every day.

✧

PSALM 19:9

The fear of the Lord is clean, enduring forever; The judgments of the Lord are true and righteous altogether.

✧

PSALM 25:22

Redeem Israel, O God, Out of all their troubles!

✧

PSALM 37:30

The mouth of the righteous speaks wisdom, And his tongue talks of justice.

✧

PSALM 37:39

But the salvation of the righteous is from the Lord; He is their strength in the time of trouble.

✧

✧

PSALM 37:40
And the Lord shall help them and deliver them; He shall deliver them from the wicked, And save them, Because they trust in Him.

✧

PSALM 46:1
God is our refuge and strength, A very present help in trouble.

✧

PSALM 51:10
Create in me a clean heart, O God, And renew a steadfast spirit within me.

✧

PSALM 75:1
We give thanks to You, O God, we give thanks! For Your wondrous works declare that Your name is near.

✧

PSALM 108:5
Be exalted, O God, above the heavens, And Your glory above all the earth;

✧

PSALM 113:4
The Lord is high above all nations, His glory above the heavens.

✧

PSALM 116:9
I will walk before the Lord In the land of the living.

✧

PSALM 118:4
Let those who fear the Lord now say, "His mercy endures forever."

✧

PSALM 118:28
You are my God, and I will praise You; You are my God, I will exalt You.

✧

PSALM 119:90
Your faithfulness endures to all generations; You established the earth, and it abides.

✧

✧

PSALM 136:26
Oh, give thanks to the God of heaven! For His mercy endures forever.

✧

PSALM 138:2
I will worship toward Your holy temple, And praise Your name For Your lovingkindness and Your truth; For You have magnified Your word above all Your name.

✧

PSALM 148:5
Let them praise the name of the Lord, For He commanded and they were created.

✧

PSALM 148:13
Let them praise the name of the Lord, For His name alone is exalted; His glory is above the earth and heaven.

✧

PSALM 150:1
Praise the Lord! Praise God in His sanctuary; Praise Him in His mighty firmament!

✧

PSALM 150:6
Let everything that has breath praise the Lord. Praise the Lord!

✧

ISAIAH 25:1
O Lord, You are my God. I will exalt You, I will praise Your name, For You have done wonderful things; Your counsels of old are faithfulness and truth.

✧

ISAIAH 25:4
For You have been a strength to the poor. A strength to the needy in his distress, A refuge from the storm, A shade from the heat; For the blast of the terrible ones is as a storm against the wall.

✧

ISAIAH 25:8

He will swallow up death forever, And the Lord God will wipe away tears from all faces; The rebuke of His people He will take away from all the earth; For the Lord has spoken.

✧

ISAIAH 40:29

He gives power to the weak, And to those who have no might He increases strength.

✧

ISAIAH 40:31

But those who wait on the Lord Shall renew their strength; They shall mount up with wings like eagles, They shall run and not be weary, They shall walk and not faint.

✧

MICAH 7:7

Therefore I will look to the Lord; I will wait for the God of my salvation; My God will hear me.

✧

MICAH 7:18

Who is a God like You, Pardoning iniquity And passing over the transgression of the remnant of His heritage? He does not retain His anger forever, Because He delights in mercy.

✧

HABAKKUK 3:19

The Lord God is my strength; He will make my feet like deer's feet, And He will make me walk on my high hills.

✧

MATTHEW 19:26

But Jesus looked at them and said to them, "With men this is impossible, but with God all things are possible."

✧

MATTHEW 21:22

"And whatever things you ask in prayer, believing, you will receive."

✧

LUKE 1:45

"Blessed is she who believed, for there will be a fulfillment of those things which were told her from the Lord."

ROMANS 15:13

Now may the God of hope fill you with all joy and peace in believing, that you may abound in hope by the power of the Holy Spirit.

I CORINTHIANS 1:3

Grace to you and peace from God our Father and the Lord Jesus Christ.

I CORINTHIANS 1:25

Because the foolishness of God is wiser than men, and the weakness of God is stronger than men.

II CORINTHIANS 5:21

For He made Him who knew no sin to be sin for us, that we might become the righteousness of God in Him.

PHILIPPIANS 1:21

For to me, to live is Christ, and to die is gain.

PHILIPPIANS 2:8

And being found in appearance as a man, He humbled Himself and became obedient to the point of death, even the death of the cross.

PHILIPPIANS 2:9

Therefore God also has highly exalted Him and given Him the name which is above every name,

PHILIPPIANS 2:10

that at the name of Jesus every knee should bow, of those in heaven, and of those on earth, and of those under the earth,

PHILIPPIANS 2:11
and that every tongue should confess that Jesus Christ is Lord, to the glory of God the Father.

PHILIPPIANS 4:4
Rejoice in the Lord always. Again I will say, rejoice!

PHILIPPIANS 4:13
I can do all things though Christ who strengthens me.

PHILIPPIANS 4:19
And my God shall supply all your need according to His riches in glory by Christ Jesus.

COLOSSIANS 1:13
He has delivered us from the power of darkness and conveyed us into the kingdom of the Son of His love.

COLOSSIANS 1:14
in whom we have redemption through His blood, the forgiveness of sins.

COLOSSIANS 1:15
He is the image of the invisible God, the firstborn over all creation.

COLOSSIANS 1:18
And He is the head of the body, the church, who is the beginning, the first-born from the dead, that in all things He may have the preeminence.

COLOSSIANS 1:19
For it pleased the Father that in Him all the fullness should dwell.

COLOSSIANS 1:20
and by Him to reconcile all things to Himself, by Him, whether things on earth or things in heaven, having made peace through the blood of His cross.

I THESSALONIANS 2:4

But as we have been approved by God to be entrusted with the gospel, even so we speak ,not as pleasing men, but God who tests our hearts.

I THESSALONIANS 2:12

that you would walk worthy of God who calls you into His own kingdom and glory.

I THESSALONIANS 2:13

For this reason we also thank God without ceasing, because when you received the word of God which you heard from us, you welcomed it not as the word of men, but as it is in truth, the word of God, which also effectively works in you who believe.

HEBREWS 1:10

And: "You, Lord, in the beginning laid the foundation of the earth, And the heavens are the work of Your hands.

HEBREWS 3:3

For this One has been counted worthy of more glory than Moses, inasmuch as He who built the house has more honor than the house.

HEBREWS 3:4

For every house is built by someone, but He who built all things is God.

JUDE 1:20

But you, beloved, building yourselves up on your most holy faith, praying in the Holy Spirit,

JUDE 1:24

Now to Him who is able to keep you from stumbling, And to present you faultless, Before the presence of His glory with exceeding joy,

JUDE 1:25

To God our Savior, Who alone is wise, Be glory and majesty, Dominion and power, Both now and forever Amen.

REVELATION 1:5

and from Jesus Christ, the faithful witness, the firstborn from the dead, and ruler over the kings of the earth. To Him who loved us and washed us from our sins in His own blood,

REVELATION 11:17

saying: "We give You thanks, O Lord God Almighty, The One who is and who was and who is to come, Because You have taken Your great power and reigned.

REVELATION 21:7

"He who overcomes shall inherit all things, and I will be his God and he shall be My son.

PSALM 135:1

Praise the Lord! Praise the name of the Lord; Praise Him, O you servants of the Lord!

I CORINTHIANS 15:57

But thanks be to God, who gives us the victory through our Lord Jesus Christ.

HEBREWS 13:6

So we may boldly say: "The Lord is my helper; I will not fear. What can man do to me?"

III JOHN 1:2

Beloved, I pray that you may prosper in all things and be in health, just as your soul prospers.

✧

JOB 5:8

"But as for me, I would seek God, And to God I would commit my cause-

✧

JOB 5:9

Who does great things, and unsearchable, Marvelous things without number.

✧

JOB 8:21

He will yet fill your mouth with laughing, And your lips with rejoicing.

✧

PSALM 84:11

For the Lord God is a sun and shield; The Lord will give grace and glory; No good thing will He withhold From those who walk uprightly.

✧

PROVERB 2:7

He stores up sound wisdom for the upright; He is a shield to those who walk uprightly;

✧

PROVERB 2:8

He guards the paths of justice, And preserves the way of His saints.

✧

PROVERB 8:11

For wisdom is better than rubies, And all the things one may desire cannot be compared with her.

✧

AMOS 4:13

For behold, He who forms mountains, And creates the wind, Who declares to man what his thought is, And makes the morning darkness, Who treads the high places of the earth- The Lord God of hosts is His name.

✧

MICAH 7:7

Therefore I will look to the Lord; I will wait for the God of my salvation; My God will hear me.

✧

NAHUM 1:4

He rebukes the sea and makes it dry, And dries up all the rivers. Bashan and Carmel wither, And the flower of Lebanon wilts.

LUKE 20:38

"For He is not the God of the dead but of the living, for all live to Him."

ACTS 5:32

"And we are His witnesses to these things, and so also is the Holy Spirit whom God has given to those who obey Him."

PSALM 28:7

The Lord is my strength and my shield; My heart trusted in Him, and I am helped; Therefore my heart greatly rejoices, And with my song I will praise Him.

PSALM 28:8

The Lord is their strength, And He is the saving refuge of His anointed.

PSALM 29:11

The Lord will give strength to His people; The Lord will bless His people with peace.

PSALM 30:12

To the end that my glory may sing praise to You and not be silent. O Lord my God, I will give thanks to You forever.

PSALM 31:1

In You, O Lord, I put my trust; Let me never be ashamed; Deliver me in Your righteousness.

PSALM 31:19

Oh, how great is Your goodness, Which You have laid up for those who fear You, Which You have prepared for those who trust in You In the presence of the sons of men!

✧

PSALM 31:20

You shall hide them in the secret place of Your presence From the plots of man; You shall keep them secretly in a pavilion From the strife of tongues.

✧

PSALM 32:7

You are my hiding place; You shall preserve me from trouble; You shall surround me with songs of deliverance. Selah.

✧

PSALM 33:4

For the word of the Lord is right, And all His work is done in truth.

✧

PSALM 33:5

He loves righteousness and justice; The earth is full of the goodness of the Lord.

✧

PSALM 33:18

Behold, the eye of the Lord is on those who fear Him, On those who hope in His mercy,

✧

PSALM 33:19

To deliver their soul from death, And to keep them alive in famine.

✧

PSALM 34:4

I sought the Lord, and He heard me, And delivered me from all my fears.

✧

PSALM 34:7

The angel of the Lord encamps all around those who fear Him, And delivers them.

✧

✧

PSALM 34:8

Oh, taste and see that the Lord is good; Blessed is the man who
trusts in Him!

✧

PSALM 34:9

Oh, fear the Lord, you His saints! There is no want to those who fear Him.

✧

PSALM 34:10

The young lions lack and suffer hunger; But those who seek the Lord shall
not lack any good thing.

✧

PSALM 34:15

The eyes of the Lord are on the righteous, And His ears are open
to their cry.

✧

PSALM 36:9

For with You is the fountain of life; In Your light we see light.

✧

PSALM 77:1

I cried out to God with my voice- To God with my voice; And He gave
ear to me.

✧

PSALM 118:14

The Lord is my strength and song, And He has become my salvation.

✧

PSALM 119:11

Your word I have hidden in my heart, That I might not sin against You.

✧

PSALM 119:30

I have chosen the way of truth; Your judgments I have
laid before me.

✧

PSALM 119:47

And I will delight myself in Your commandments, Which I love.

✧

PSALM 119:50
This is my comfort in my affliction, For Your word has given me life.

PSALM 119:105
Your word is a lamp to my feet And a light to my path.

PSALM 119:130
The entrance of Your words gives light; It gives understanding to the simple.

PSALM 119:160
The entirety of Your word is truth, And every one of Your righteous judgements endures forever.

PSALM 119:162
I rejoice at Your word As one who finds great treasure.

PSALM 119:164
Seven times a day I praise You, Because of Your righteous judgments.

PSALM 121:2
My help comes from the Lord, Who made heaven and earth.

PSALM 121:3
He will not allow your foot to be moved; He who keeps you will not slumber.

PSALM 121:7
The Lord shall preserve you from all evil; He shall preserve your soul.

PSALM 124:8
Our help is in the name of the Lord, Who made heaven and earth.

PSALM 125:1
Those who trust in the Lord Are like Mount Zion, Which cannot be moved, but abides forever.

PSALM 125:2
As the mountain surround Jerusalem, So the Lord surrounds His people From this time forth forever.

PSALM 128:1
Blessed is every one who fears the Lord, Who walks in His ways.

PSALM 128:4
Behold, thus shall the man be blessed Who fears the Lord.

PSALM 136:26
Oh, give thanks to the God of heaven! For His mercy endures forever.

PSALM 138:3
In the day when I cried out, You answered me, And made me bold with strength in my soul.

PSALM 138:8
The Lord will perfect that which concerns me; Your mercy, O Lord, endures forever; Do not forsake the works of Your hands.

PSALM 147:5
Great is our Lord, and mighty in power; His understanding is infinite.

JEREMIAH 17:7
Blessed is the man who trusts in the Lord, And whose hope is the Lord.

LAMENTATIONS 3:22
Through the Lord's mercies we are not consumed, Because His compassions fail not.

✧

LAMENTATIONS 3:23
They are new every morning; Great is Your faithfulness.

✧

DANIEL 9:19
"O Lord, hear! O Lord, forgive! O Lord, listen and act! Do not delay for Your own sake, my God, for Your city and Your people are called by Your name."

✧

LUKE 21:15
"for I will give you a mouth and wisdom which all your adversaries willl not be able to contradict or resist.

✧

JOHN 6:35
And Jesus said to them, "I am the bread of life. He who comes to Me shall never hunger, and he who believes in Me shall never thirst.

✧

JOHN 6:37
"All that the Father gives Me will come to Me, and the one who comes to Me I will by no means cast out.

✧

ACTS 3:26
"To you first, God, having raised up His Servant Jesus, sent Him to bless you, in turning away every one of you from your iniquities."

✧

ACTS 11:24
For He was a good man, full of the Holy Spirit and of faith. And a great many people were added to the Lord.

✧

ACTS 13:48
Now when the Gentiles heard this, they were glad and glorified the word of the Lord. And as many as had been appointed to eternal life believed.

✧

I CORINTHIANS 15:20
But now Christ is risen from the dead, and has become the firstfruits of those who have fallen asleep.

I CORINTHIANS 15:22

For as in Adam all die, even so in Christ all shall be made alive.

I CORINTHIANS 15:25

For He must reign till He has put all enemies under His feet.

I CORINTHIANS 15:54

So when this corruptible has put on incorruption, and this mortal has put on immortality, then shall be brought to pass the saying that is written: "Death is swallowed up in victory."

II CORINTHIANS 4:14

knowing that He who raised up the Lord Jesus will also raise us up with Jesus, and will present us with you.

II CORINTHIANS 4:16

Therefore we do not lose heart. Even though our outward man is perishing, yet the inward man is being renewed day by day.

II CORINTHIANS 8:9

For you know the grace of our Lord Jesus Christ, that though He was rich, yet for your sakes He became poor, that you through His poverty might become rich.

II CORINTHIANS 13:4

For though He was crucified in weakness, yet He lives by the power of God. For we also are weak in Him, but we shall live with Him by the power of God toward you.

GALATIANS 2:20

"I have been crucified with Christ; it is no longer I who live, but Christ lives in me; and that life which I now live in the flesh I live by faith in the Son of God, who loved me and gave Himself for me.

✧

GALATIANS 3:29

And if you are Christ's, then you are Abraham's seed, and heirs according
to the promise.

✧

GALATIANS 4:7

Therefore you are no longer a slave but a son, and if a son, then an heir of
God through Christ.

✧

GALATIANS 4:31

So then, brethren, we are not children of the bondwoman but of the free.

✧

PHILIPPIANS 4:19

And my God shall supply all your need according to His riches in glory
by Christ Jesus.

✧

COLOSSIANS 1:19

For it pleased the Father that in Him all the fullness should dwell,

✧

COLOSSIANS 1:20

and by Him to reconcile all things to Himself, by Him, whether things on
earth or things in heaven, having made peace through the blood
of His cross.

✧

I THESSALONIANS 5:5

You are all sons of the light and sons of the day. We are not of the night
nor of darkness.

✧

I TIMOTHY 2:5

For there is one God and one Mediator between God and men, the Man
Christ Jesus,

✧

I TIMOTHY 2:6

who gave Himself a ransom for all, to be testified in due time,

✧

⟡

I PETER 3:12

For the eyes of the Lord are on the righteous, And His ears are open to their prayers; But the face of the Lord is against those who do evil."

⟡

I JOHN 4:12

No one has seen God at any time. If we love one another, God abides in us, and His love has been perfected in us.

⟡

I JOHN 5:14

Now this is the confidence, that we have in Him, that if we ask anything according to His will, He hears us.

⟡

I JOHN 5:15

And if we know that He hears us, whatever we ask, we know that we have the petitions that we have asked of Him.

⟡

REVELATION 21:7

"He who overcomes shall inherit all things, and I will be his God and He shall be My son.

⟡

REVELATION 22:14

Blessed are those who do His commandments, that they may have the right to the tree of life, and may enter through the gates into the city.

⟡

Gods Command

✧

EXODUS 20:3
"You shall have no other gods before Me.

✧

EXODUS 20:7
"You shall not take the name of the Lord your God in vain, for the Lord will not hold him guiltless who takes His name in vain.

✧

DEUTERONOMY 10:20
"You shall fear the Lord your God; you shall serve Him, and to Him you shall hold fast, and take oaths in His name.

✧

MARK 16:16
"He who believes and is baptized will be saved; but He who does not believe will be condemned.

✧

MARK 16:17
"And these signs will follow those who believe: In My name they will cast out demons; they will speak with new tongues;

✧

MARK 16:18
"they will take up serpents; and if they drink anything deadly, it will by no means hurt them; they will lay hands on the sick, and they will recover."

✧

LUKE 4:18
The Spirit of the Lord is upon Me, Because He has anointed Me To preach the gospel to the poor; He has sent Me to heal the brokenhearted, To proclaim liberty to the captives And recovery of sight to the blind, To set at liberty those who are oppressed;

✧

LUKE 6:36
"Therefore be merciful, just as your Father also is merciful.

✧

LUKE 6:37
"Judge not, and you shall not be judged. Condemn not, and you shall not be condemned. Forgive, and you will be forgiven.

✧

LUKE 9:56
"For the Son of Man did not come to destroy men's lives but to save them."

✧

LUKE 12:8
"Also I say to you, whoever confesses Me before men, him the Son of Man also will confess before the angels of God.

✧

LUKE 12:9
"But he who denies Me before men will be denied before the angels of God.

✧

ACTS 13:47
"For so the Lord has commanded us: 'I have set you as a light to the Gentiles, That you should be for salvation to the ends of the earth.' "

✧

ACTS 13:48
Now when the Gentiles heard this, they were glad and glorified the word of the Lord. And as many as had been appointed to eternal life believed.

✧

ACTS 14:27
Now when they had come and gathered the church together, they reported all that God had done with them, and that He had opened the door of faith to the Gentiles.

✧

ACTS 15:8
"So God, who knows the heart, acknowledged them by giving them the Holy Spirit, just as He did to us,

✧

ACTS 16:29

Then He called for a light, ran in, and fell down trembling before Paul and Silas.

✧

ACTS 16:30

And he brought them out and said, "Sirs, what must I do to be saved?"

✧

ACTS 16:31

So they said, "Believe on the Lord Jesus Christ, and you will be saved, you and your household."

✧

I CORINTHIANS 6:17

But he who is joined to the Lord is one spirit with Him.

✧

I CORINTHIANS 6:20

For you were bought at a price; therefore glorify God in your body and in your spirit, which are God's.

✧

ISAIAH 12:4

And in that day you will say: "Praise the Lord; call upon His name; Declare His deeds among the peoples, Make mention that His name is exalted.

✧

LAMENTATIONS 3:40

Let us search out and examine our ways, And turn back to the Lord;

✧

LAMENTATIONS 3:41

Let us lift our hearts and hands To God in heaven.

✧

MARK 12:30

'And you shall love the Lord your God with all your heart, with all your soul, with all your mind, and with all your strength.' This is the first commandment.

✧

MARK 12:31

"And the second, like it, is this: 'You shall love your neighbor as yourself.'
There is no other commandment greater than these."

✧

MARK 13:10

"And the gospel must first be preached to all the nations.

✧

ROMANS 6:11

Likewise you also, reckon yourselves to be dead indeed to sin, but alive to
God in Christ Jesus our Lord.

✧

ROMANS 6:12

Therefore do not let sin reign in your mortal body, that you should obey it
in its lusts.

✧

ROMANS 6:14

For sin shall not have dominion over you, for you are not under law but
under grace.

✧

I THESSALONIANS 1:2

We give thanks to God always for you all, making mention of you
in our prayers,

✧

II CHRONICLES 7:14

"if My people who are called by My name will humble themselves, and
pray and seek My face, and turn from their wicked ways, then I will hear
from heaven, and will forgive their sin and heal their land.

✧

II CHRONICLES 18:13

And Micaiah said, "As the Lord lives, whatever my God says, that
will I speak."

✧

II CHRONICLES 20:15

And he said, "Listen, all you of Judah and you inhabitants of Jerusalem, and you, King Jehoshaphat! Thus says the Lord to you: 'Do not be afraid nor dismayed because of this great multitude, for the battle is not yours, but God's.

NEHEMIAH 4:14

And I looked, and arose and said to the nobles, to the leaders, and to the rest of the people, "Do not be afraid of them. Remember the Lord, great and awesome, and fight for your brethren, your sons, your daughters, your wives, and your houses."

PSALM 66:18

If I regard iniquity in my heart, The Lord will not hear.

PSALM 122:6

Pray for the peace of Jerusalem: "May they prosper who love you.

PSALM 122:7

Peace be within your walls, Prosperity within your palaces."

PROVERBS 4:1

Hear, my children, the instruction of a father, And give attention to know understanding;

PROVERBS 4:24

Put away from you a deceitful mouth, And put perverse lips far from you.

PROVERBS 5:7

Therefore hear me now, my children, And do not depart from the words of my mouth.

PROVERBS 7:1

My son, keep my words, And treasure my commands within you, Keep my commands and live, And my law as the apple of your eye.

✧

PROVERBS 7:24

Now therefore, listen to me, my children; Pay attention to the words of my mouth:

✧

PROVERBS 22:24

Make no friendship with an angry man, And with a furious man do not go,

✧

PROVERBS 22:26

Do not be one of these who shakes hands in a pledge, One of those who is surety for debts;

✧

PROVERBS 23:17

Do not let your heart envy sinners, but be zealous for the fear of the Lord all the day;

✧

PROVERBS 24:17

Do not rejoice when your enemy falls, And do not let your heart be glad when he stumbles;

✧

PROVERBS 24:18

Lest the Lord see it, and it displease Him, And He turn away His wrath from him.

✧

PROVERBS 24:28

Do not be a witness against your neighbor without cause, For would you deceive with your lips?

✧

PROVERBS 30:6

Do not add to His words, Lest He rebuke you, and you be found a liar.

✧

ECCLESIASTES 5:2

Do not be rash with your mouth, And let not your heart utter anything hastily before God. For God is in heaven, and you on earth; Therefore let your words be few.

✧

ECCLESIASTES 5:6

Do not let your mouth cause your flesh to sin, nor say before the messenger of God, that it was an error. Why should God be angry at your excuse and destroy the work of your hands?

ECCLESIASTES 12:13

Let us hear the conclusion of the whole matter: Fear God and keep His commandments. For this is man's all.

ISAIAH 1:17

Learn to do good; Seek justice, Rebuke the oppressor; Defend the fatherless, Plead for the widow.

ISAIAH 12:5

Sing to the Lord, For He has done excellent things; This is known in all the earth.

ISAIAH 32:17

The work of righteousness will be peace, And the effect of righteousness, quietness and assurance forever.

ISAIAH 40:1

"Comfort, yes, comfort my people!" says your God.

ISAIAH 40:2

"Speak comfort to Jerusalem, and cry out to her, That her warfare is ended, That her iniquity is pardoned; For she has received from the Lord's hand Double for all her sins."

ISAIAH 40:5

The glory of the Lord shall be revealed, And all flesh shall see it together; For the mouth of the Lord has spoken."

ISAIAH 41:10

Fear not, for I am with you; Be not dismayed, for I am your God, I will strengthen you, Yes, I will help you, I will uphold you with My righteous right hand.'

✧

ISAIAH 41:13

For I, the Lord your God, will hold your right hand, Saying to you, 'Fear not, I will help you.'

✧

ISAIAH 43:18

Do not remember the former things, Nor consider the things of old.

✧

ISAIAH 43:26

Put Me in remembrance; Let us contend together; State your case, that you may be acquitted.

✧

ISAIAH 44:6

"Thus says the Lord, the King of Israel, And his Redeemer, the Lord of hosts: 'I am the First and I am the Last; Besides Me there is no God.

✧

ISAIAH 44:8

Do not fear, nor be afraid; Have I not told you from that time, and declared it? You are My witnesses. Is there a God besides me? Indeed there is no other Rock; I know not one.'"

✧

ISAIAH 44:24

Thus says the Lord, your redeemer, And He who formed you from the womb: "I am the Lord, who mades all things, Who stretches out the heavens all alone, Who spreads abroad the earth by Myself;

✧

ISAIAH 45:11

Thus says the Lord, The Holy One of Israel, and his Maker: Ask of things to come concerning My sons; And concerning the work of My hands, you command Me.

✧

ISAIAH 48:11

For My own sake, for My own sake, I will do it; For how should My name be profaned? And I will not give My glory to another.

✧

ISAIAH 48:12

"Listen to Me, O Jacob, And Israel, My called: I am He, I am the First, I am also the Last.

✧

ISAIAH 51:4

"Listen to Me, My people; And give ear to Me, O My nation: For law will proceed from Me, And I will make My justice rest As a light of the peoples.

✧

ISAIAH 51:7

"Listen to Me, you who know righteousness, You people in whose heart is My law: Do not fear the reproach of men, Nor be afraid of their insults.

✧

ISAIAH 55:6

Seek the Lord while He may be found, Call upon Him while He is near.

✧

ISAIAH 65:17

"For behold, I create new heavens and a new earth; And the former shall not be remembered or come to mind.

✧

ISAIAH 66:23

And it shall come to pass That from one New Moon to another, And from one Sabbath to another, All flesh shall come to worship before Me," says the Lord.

✧

JEREMIAH 1:7

But the Lord said to me: "Do not say, 'I am a youth,' For you shall go to all to whom I send you, And whatever I command you, you shall speak.

✧

JEREMIAH 7:23

"But this is what I command them, saying, 'Obey My voice and I will be your God, and you shall be My people. And walk in all the ways that I have commanded you, that it may be well with you.'

✧

EZEKIEL 18:31

"Cast away from you all the transgressions which you have committed, and get yourselves a new heart and a new spirit. For why should you die, O house of Israel?

✧

EZEKIEL 18:32

"For I have no pleasure in the death of one who dies," says the Lord God. "Therefore turn and live!"

✧

EZEKIEL 20:19

'I am the Lord your God: Walk in My statutes, keep My judgments, and do them;

✧

HOSEA 13:4

"Yet I am the Lord your God Ever since the land of Egypt, and you shall know no God but Me; For there is no savior besides Me.

✧

AMOS 5:14

Seek good and not evil, That you may live; So the Lord God of hosts will be with you, As you have spoken.

✧

AMOS 5:15

Hate evil, love good; Establish justice in the gate. It may be that the Lord God of hosts Will be gracious to the remnant of Joseph.

✧

MICAH 7:5

Do not trust in a friend. Do not put your confidence in a companion; Guard the doors of your mouth From her who lies in your bosom.

✧

ZEPHANIAH 2:3

Seek the Lord, all you meek of the earth, Who have upheld His justice. Seek righteousness, seek humility. It may be that you will be hidden, In the day of the LORD'S anger.

✧

ZECHARIAH 7:9

"Thus says the Lord of hosts: 'Execute true justice, Show mercy and compassion Everyone to his brother.

ZECHARIAH 7:10

Do not oppress the widow or the fatherless, The alien or the poor. Let none of you plan evil in his heart Against his brother.'

ZECHARIAH 8:16

These are the things you shall do: Speak each man the truth to his neighbor; Give judgment in your gates for truth, justice, and peace;

ZECHARIAH 8:17

Let none of you think evil in your heart against your neighbor; And do not love a false oath. For all these are things that I hate,' Says the Lord."

MALACHI 1:14

"But cursed be the deceiver Who has in his flock a male, And takes a vow, But sacrifices to the Lord what is blemished- For I am a great King," Says the Lord of hosts, "And My name is to be feared among the nations.

MATTHEW 6:33

"But seek first the kingdom of God and His righteousness, and all these things shall be added to you.

MATTHEW 7:1

"Judge not, that you be not judged.

MATTHEW 9:13

"But go and learn what this means: 'I desire mercy and not sacrifice.' For I did not come to call the righteous, but sinners, to repentance."

MATTHEW 11:28

"Come to Me, all you who labor and are heavy laden, and I will give you rest.

MATTHEW 15:4

"For God commanded, saying, 'Honor your father and your mother' and, 'He who curses father or mother, let him be put to death.'

MATTHEW 22:37

Jesus said to him, "You shall love the Lord your God with all your heart, with all your soul, and with all your mind.'

MATTHEW 22:39

"And the second is like it: 'You shall love your neighbor as yourself.'

MATTHEW 22:40

"On these two commandments hang all the Law and the Prophets."

MATTHEW 22:32

'I am the God of Abraham, the God of Isaac, and the God of Jacob? God is not the God of the dead, but of the living."

MATTHEW 24:35

"Heaven and earth will pass away, but My words will by no means pass away.

MATTHEW 28:18

And Jesus came and spoke to them, saying "All authority has been given to Me in heaven and on earth.

LUKE 6:27

"But I say to you who hear: Love your enemies, do good to those who hate you,

LUKE 6:28

"bless those who curse you, and pray for those who spitefully use you.

LUKE 12:5

"But I will show you whom you should fear: Fear Him who, after He has killed, has power to cast into hell; yes, I say to you, fear Him!

LUKE 12:31

"But seek the kingdom of God, and all these things shall be added to you.

LUKE 13:24

"Strive to enter through the narrow gate, for many, I say to you, will seek to enter and will not be able.

LUKE 17:6

So the Lord said, "If you have faith as a mustard seed, you can say to this mulberry tree, 'Be pulled up by the roots and be planted in the sea,' and it would obey you.

LUKE 24:47

"and that repentance and remission of sins should be preached in His name to all nations, beginning at Jerusalem.

JOHN 14:1

"Let not your heart be troubled; you believe in God, believe also in Me.

JOHN 14:6

Jesus said to Him, "I am the way, the truth, and the life. No one comes to the Father except through Me.

JOHN 14:15

"If you love Me, keep My commandments.

JOHN 15:12

"This is My commandment that you love one another as I have loved you.

✧

JOHN 15:14
"You are My friends if you do whatever I command you.

✧

ACTS 3:19
"Repent therefore and be converted, that your sins may be blotted out, so that times of refreshing may come from the presence of the Lord,

✧

ACTS 3:25
"You are sons of the prophets, and of the covenant which God made with our fathers, saying to Abraham, 'And in your seed all the families of the earth shall be blessed.'

✧

ROMANS 6:12
Therefore do not let sin reign in your mortal body, that you should obey it in its lusts.

✧

ROMANS 6:14
For sin shall not have dominion over you, for you are not under law but under grace.

✧

ROMANS 12:17
Repay no one evil for evil. Have regard for good things in the sight of all men.

✧

ROMANS 12:18
If it is possible, as much as depends on you, live peaceably with all men.

✧

ROMANS 12:19
Beloved do not avenge yourself, but rather give place to wrath; for it is written, "Vengeance is Mine, I will repay," says the Lord.

✧

ROMANS 14:19
Therefore let us pursue the things which make for peace and the things by which one may edify another.

✧

✧

I CORINTHIANS 7:23
You were bought at a price; do not become slaves of men.

✧

I CORINTHIANS 10:26
for "the earth is the Lord's and all its fullness."

✧

I CORINTHIANS 10:31
Therefore, whether you eat or drink, or whatever you do, do all to the glory of God.

✧

I CORINTHIANS 11:31
For if we would judge ourselves, we would not be judged.

✧

II CORINTHIANS 6:14
Do not be unequally yoked together with unbelievers. For what fellowship has righteousness with lawlessness? And what communion has light with darkness?

✧

II CORINTHIANS 6:17
Therefore "Come out from among them And be separate, says the Lord, Do not touch what is unclean, And I will receive you."

✧

II CORINTHIANS 6:18
"I will be a Father to you, And you shall be My sons and daughters, Says the LORD Almighty."

✧

GALATIANS 5:1
Stand fast therefore in the liberty by which Christ has made us free, and do not be entangled again with the yoke of bondage.

✧

GALATIANS 5:25
If we live in the Spirit, let us also walk in the Spirit.

✧

GALATIANS 6:4
But let each one examine his own work, and then he will have rejoicing in himself alone, and not in another.

GALATIANS 6:9
And let us not grow weary while doing good, for in due season we shall reap if we do not lose heart.

GALATIANS 6:10
Therefore, as we have opportunity, let us do good to all, especially to those who are of the household of faith.

EPHESIANS 4:14
that we should no longer be children, tossed to and fro and carried about with every wind of doctrine, by the trickery of men, in the cunning craftiness of deceitful plotting,

EPHESIANS 4:15
but, speaking the truth in love, may grow up in all things into Him who is the head-Christ-

EPHESIANS 4:21
if indeed you have heard Him and have been taught by Him, as the truth is in Jesus:

EPHESIANS 4:22
that you put off, concerning your former conduct, the old man which grows corrupt according to the deceitful lusts,

EPHESIANS 4:23
and be renewed in the spirit of your mind,

EPHESIANS 4:24
and that you put on the new man, which was created according to God, in true righteousness and holiness.

EPHESIANS 4:25
Therefore, putting away lying, "Let each one of you speak truth with his neighbor," for we are members of one another.

EPHESIANS 4:26
"Be angry, and do not sin" do not let the sun go down on your wrath,

EPHESIANS 4:29
Let no corrupt word proceed out of your mouth, but what is good for necessary edification, that it may impart grace to the hearers.

EPHESIANS 4:20
But you have not so learned Christ,.

EPHESIANS 5:8
For you were once darkness, but now you are light in the Lord. Walk as children of light

EPHESIANS 5:9
(for the fruit of the Spirit is in all goodness, righteousness, and truth),

EPHESIANS 6:1
Children, obey your parents in the Lord, for this is right.

EPHESIANS 6:2
"Honor your father and mother," which is the first commandment with promise:

EPHESIANS 6:3
"that it may be well with you and you may live long on the earth."

EPHESIANS 6:10
Finally, my brethren, be strong in the Lord and in the power of His might.

✧

EPHESIANS 6:11

Put on the whole armor of God, that you may be able to stand against the wiles of the devil.

✧

EPHESIANS 6:13

Therefore take up the whole armor of God, that you may be able to withstand in the evil day, and having done all, to stand.

✧

EPHESIANS 6:16

above all, taking the shield of faith with which you will be able to quench all the fiery darts of the wicked one.

✧

EPHESIANS 6:17

And take the helmet of salvation, and the sword of the spirit, which is the word of God;

✧

PHILIPPIANS 2:11

and that every tongue should confess that Jesus Christ is Lord, to the glory of God the Father.

✧

PHILIPPIANS 4:6

Be anxious for nothing, but in everything by prayer and supplication, with thanksgiving, let your requests be made known to God;

✧

PHILIPPIANS 4:9

The things which you learned and received and heard and saw in me, these do, and the God of peace will be with you.

✧

COLOSSIANS 2:6

As you therefore have received Christ Jesus the Lord, so walk in Him,

✧

COLOSSIANS 2:9

For in Him dwells all the fullness of the Godhead bodily;

✧

✧

COLOSSIANS 2:10

and you are complete in Him, who is the head of all principality and power.

✧

COLOSSIANS 3:1

If then you were raised with Christ, seek those things which are above,
where Christ is, sitting at the right hand of God.

✧

COLOSSIAN 3:2

Set your mind on things above, not on things on the earth.

✧

COLOSSIANS 3:3

For you died, and your life is hidden with Christ in God.

✧

COLOSSIANS 3:14

But above all these things put on love, which is the bond of perfection.

✧

COLOSSIANS 3:15

And let the peace of God rule in your hearts, to which also you were called
in one body: and be thankful.

✧

COLOSSIANS 3:17

And whatever you do in word or deed, do all in the name of the Lord Jesus,
giving thanks to God the Father through Him.

✧

COLOSSIANS 3:23

And whatever you do, do it heartily, as to the Lord and not to men,

✧

COLOSSIANS 4:5

Walk in wisdom toward those who are outside, redeeming the time.

✧

COLOSSIANS 4:6

Let your speech always be with grace, seasoned with salt, that you may
know how you ought to answer each one.

✧

✧

I THESSALONIANS 5:16
Rejoice always,

✧

I THESSALONIANS 5:18
in everything give thanks; for this is the will of God in Christ Jesus for you.

✧

I THESSALONIANS 5:21
Test all things; hold fast what is good.

✧

II THESSALONIANS 2:13
But we are bound to give thanks to God always for you, brethren beloved by the Lord, because God from the beginning chose you for salvation through santification by the Spirit and belief in the truth,

✧

II THESSALONIANS 3:10
For even when we were with you, we commanded you this: If anyone will not work, neither shall he eat.

✧

II THESSALONIANS 3:13
But as for you, brethren, do not grow weary in doing good.

✧

I TIMOTHY 2:1
Therefore I exhort first of all that supplications, prayers, intercessions, and giving of thanks be made for all men,

✧

I TIMOTHY 2:8
I desire therefore that the men pray everywhere, lifting up holy hands, without wrath and doubting;

✧

I TIMOTHY 6:12
Fight the good fight of faith, lay hold on eternal life, to which you were also called and have confessed the good confession in the presence of many witnesses.

✧

II TIMOTHY 1:13
Hold fast the pattern of sound words which you have heard from me, in faith and love which are in Christ Jesus.

II TIMOTHY 2:7
Consider what I say, and may the Lord give you understanding in all things.

TITUS 2:1
But as for you, speak the things which are proper for sound doctrine:

HEBREWS 3:1
Therefore, holy brethren, partakers of the heavenly calling, consider the Apostle and High Priest of our confession, Christ Jesus.

HEBREWS 4:16
Let us therefore come boldly to the throne of grace, that we may obtain mercy and find grace to help in time of need.

HEBREWS 7:17
For He testifies: "You are priest forever According to the order of Mel-chizedeck."

HEBREWS 12:14
Pursue peace with all people, and holiness, without which no one will see the Lord:

HEBREWS 12:29
For our God is a consuming fire.

HEBREWS 13:5
Let your conduct be without covetousness; be content with such things as you have. For He Himself has said, "I will never leave you nor forsake you."

JAMES 2:17
Thus also faith by itself, if it does not have works, is dead.

JAMES 2:24
You see then that a man is justified by works, and not by faith only.

I JOHN 4:11
Beloved, if God so loved us, we also ought to love one another.

I JOHN 4:21
And this commandment we have from Him: that he who loves God must love his brother also.

III JOHN 1:11
Beloved, do not imitate what is evil, but what is good. He who does good is of God, but he who does evil has not seen God.

JUDE 1:2
Mercy, peace, and love be multiplied to you.

PSALM 100:4
Enter into His gates with thanksgiving, And into His courts with praise. Be thankful to Him, and bless His name.

PSALM 37:3
Trust in the Lord, and do good: Dwell in the land, and feed on His faithfulness.

PSALM 37:4
Delight yourself also in the Lord; And He shall give you the desires of your heart.

PROVERB 1:33
But whoever listens to me will dwell safely, And will be secure, without fear of evil."

PROVERB 3:5

Trust in the Lord with all your heart, And lean not on your own understanding;

✧

PROVERB 3:6

In all your ways acknowledge Him, And He shall direct your paths.

✧

PROVERB 12:26

The righteous should choose his friends carefully, For the way of the wicked leads them astry.

✧

PROVERB 24:17

Do not rejoice when your enemy falls, And do not let your heart be glad when he stumbles;

✧

PROVERB 24:18

Lest the Lord see it, and it displease Him, And He turn away His wrath from Him.

✧

ISAIAH 2:4

He shall judge between the nations, And rebuke many people; They shall beat their swords into plowshares, And their spears into prunung hooks; Nation shall not lift up sword against nation, Neither shall they learn war anymore.

✧

MICAH 6:8

He has shown you, O man, what is good; And what does the Lord require of you But to do justly, to love mercy, And to walk humbly with your God?

✧

MALACHI 3:6

"For I am the Lord, I do not change; Therefore you are not consumed, O sons of Jacob.

✧

MATTHEW 5:21

"You have heard that it was said to those of old, 'You shall not murder, and whoever murders will be in danger of the judgment.'

MATTHEW 5:22

"But I say to you that whoever is angry with his brother without a cause shall be in danger of the judgment.

MATTHEW 7:2

"For with what judgment you judge, you will be judged; and with the measure you use, it will be measured back to you.

GALATIANS 5:14

For all the law is fulfilled in one word, even in this. "You shall love your neighbor as yourself."

GALATIANS 5:16

I say then: Walk in the Spirit, and you shall not fulfill the lust of the flesh.

GALATIANS 5:22

But the fruit of the Spirit is love, joy, peace, longsuffering, kindness, goodness, faithfulness.

GALATIANS 5:23

gentleness, self control. Against such there is no law.

GALATIANS 5:24

And those who are Christ's have crucified the flesh with its passions and desires.

I PETER 3:11

Let him turn away from evil and do good; Let him seek peace and pursue it.

I JOHN 3:23

And this is His commandment: that we should believe on the name of His Son Jesus Christ and love one another, as He gave us commandment.

I JOHN 4:11

Beloved, if God so loved us, we also ought to love one another.

I JOHN 4:21

And this commandment we have from Him: that he who love God must love His brother also.

REVELATION 21:8

"But the cowardly, unbelieving, abominable, murderers, sexually immoral, sorcerers, idolaters, and all liars shall have their part in the lake which burns with fire and brimstone, which is the second death."

REVELATION 21:27

But there shall by no means enter it anything that defiles, or causes an abomination or a lie, but only those who are written in the Lamb's Book of Life.

REVELATION 22:18

For I testify to everyone who hears the words of the prophecy of this book: If anyone adds to these things, God will add to him the plagues that are written in this book;

REVELATION 22:19

and if anyone takes away from the words of the book of this prophecy, God shall take away his part from the Book of Life, from the holy city, and from the things which are written in this book.

God's Mercy and Wisdom

✧

PSALM 9:9
The Lord also will be a refuge for the oppressed, A refuge in times of trouble.

✧

PSALM 89:34
My covenant I will not break, Nor alter the word that has gone out of My lips.

✧

PSALM 89:35
Once I have sworn by My holiness; I will not lie to David:

✧

PSALM 91:9
Because you have made the LORD, who is my refuge, Even the Most High, your dwelling place,

✧

PSALM 91:10
No evil shall befall you, Nor shall any plague come near your dwelling;

✧

PSALM 91:11
For He shall give His angels charge over you, To keep you in all your ways.

✧

PSALM 91:14
"Because he has set his love upon Me, therefore I will deliver him; I will set him on high, because he has known My name.

✧

PSALM 91:15
He shall call upon Me, and I will answer him; I will be with him in trouble; I will deliver him and honor him.

✧

PSALM 93:4

The LORD on high is mightier Than the noise of many waters, Than the mighty waves of the sea.

ZEPHANIAH 3:5

The Lord is righteous in her midst, He will do no unrighteousness, Every morning He brings His justice to light; He never fails, But the unjust knows no shame.

ZEPHANIAH 3:12

I will leave in your midst A meek and humble people, And they shall trust in the name of the Lord.

MATTHEW 10:32

"Therefore whoever confesses Me before men, him I will also confess before My Father who is in heaven.

MATTHEW 10:33

"But whoever denies Me before men, him I will also deny before My Father who is in heaven.

JOHN 3:17

"For God did not send His Son into the world to condemn the world, but that the world through Him might be saved.

JOHN 3:18

"He who believes in Him is not condemned; but he who does not believe is condemned already, because he has not believed in the name of the only begotten Son of God.

JOHN 3:33

"He who has received His testimony has certified that God is true.

JOHN 3:36

"He who believes in the Son has everlasting life; and he who does not believe the Son shall not see life, but the wrath of God abides on him."

JOHN 5:20

"For the Father loves the Son, and shows Him all things that He Himself does; and He will show Him greater works than these, that you may marvel.

PSALM 107:29

He calms the Storm, so that its waves are still.

PSALM 39:1

I said, "I will guard my ways, Lest I sin with my tongue; I will restrain my mouth with a muzzle, While the wicked are before me."

PSALM 119:66

Teach me good judgment and knowledge, For I believe Your commandments.

The Lord Will Fight For You

Wisdom and Knowledge

✧

PSALM 9:10
And those who know Your name will put their trust in You; For You, Lord, have not forsaken those who seek You.

✧

PSALM 18:30
As for God, His way is perfect; The word of the Lord is proven; He is a shield to all who trust in Him.

✧

PSALM 103:19
The Lord has established His throne in heaven, And His kingdom rules over all.

✧

PSALM 94:1
O Lord God, to whom vengeance belongs- O God, to whom vengeance belongs, shine forth!

✧

PSALM 94:2
Rise up, O judge of the earth; Render punishment to the proud.

✧

PSALM 94:11
The Lord knows the thoughts of man, That they are futile.

✧

PSALM 96:13
For He is coming, for He is coming to judge the earth. He shall judge the world with righteousness, And the people with His truth.

✧

PSALM 97:2
Clouds and darkness surround Him; Righteousness and justice are the foundation of His throne.

✧

PSALM 97:9

For You, Lord, are most high above all the earth; You are exalted far above all gods.

✧

ISAIAH 64:8

But now, O Lord, You are our Father; We are the clay, and You our potter; And all we are the work of Your hand.

✧

ISAIAH 66:16

For by fire and by His sword The Lord will judge all flesh; And the slain of the Lord shall be many.

✧

EZEKIEL 16:6

"And when I passed by you and saw you struggling in your own blood, I said to you in your blood, 'Live!' Yes, I said to you in your blood, 'Live!'

✧

JOEL 2:32

And it shall come to pass That whoever calls on the name of the LORD Shall be saved, For in Mount Zion and in Jerusalem there shall be deliverance, As Lord has said, Among the remnant whom the Lord calls.

✧

MATTHEW 15:11

"Not what goes into the mouth defiles a man; but what comes out of the mouth, this defiles a man."

✧

MATTHEW 15:18

"But those things which proceed out of the mouth come from the heart, and they defile a man.

✧

MATTHEW 15:19

"For out of the heart proceed evil thoughts, murders, adulteries, fornication, thefts, false witness, blasphemies.

✧

MATTHEW 15:20

"These are the things which defile a man, but to eat with unwashed hands does not defile a man."

MATTHEW 17:20

So Jesus said to them, "Because of your unbelief; for assuredly, I say to you, if you have faith as a mustard seed, you will say to this mountain, 'Move from here to there,' and it will move; and nothing will be impossible for you.

MATTHEW 18:19

"Again I say to you that if two of you agree on earth concerning anything that they ask, it will be done for them by My Father in heaven.

MATTHEW 18:20

"For when two or three are gathered together in My name, I am there in the midst of them."

MATTHEW 19:6

"So then, they are no longer two but one flesh. Therefore what God has joined together, let not man separate."

MARK 1:4

John came baptizing in the wilderness and preaching a baptism of repentance for the remission of sins.

MARK 1:8

"I indeed baptize you with water, but He will baptize you with the Holy Spirit."

MARK 3:28

"Assuredly, I say to you, all sins will be forgiven the sons of men, and whatever blasphemies they may utter;

MARK 3:29
"but He who blasphemes against the Holy Spirit never has forgiveness, but is subject to eternal condemnation"

JOHN 5:22
"For the Father judges no one, but has committed all judgment to the Son,

JOHN 5:24
"Most assuredly, I say to you, he who hears My word and believes in Him who sent Me has everlasting life, and shall not come into judgment, but has passed from death into life.

JOHN 5:30
"I can of Myself do nothing. As I hear, I judge; and My judgment is righteous, because I do not seek My own will but the will of the Father who sent Me.

JOHN 6:38
"For I have come down from heaven, not to do My own will, but the will of Him who sent Me.

JOHN 6:47
"Most assuredly, I say to you, he who believes in Me has everlasting life.

JOHN 6:48
"I am the bread of life.

JOHN 6:50
"This is the bread which comes down from heaven, that one may eat of it and not die.

JOHN 8:51
"Most assuredly, I say to you, if anyone keeps My word he shall never see death. "

JOHN 10:10

"The thief does not come except to steal, and to kill, and to destroy. I have come that they may have life, and that they may have it more abundantly.

✧

JOHN 14:16

"And I will pray the Father, and He will give you another Helper, that He may abide with you forever-

✧

JOHN 15:23

"He who hates Me hates My Father also.

✧

ACTS 10:34

Then Peter opened his mouth and said: "In truth I perceive that God shows no partiality.

✧

ACTS 10:35

"But in every nation whoever fears Him and works righteousness is accepted by Him.

✧

ACTS 10:36

"The word which God sent to the children of Israel, preaching peace through Jesus Christ- He is Lord of all-

✧

ACT 10:42

"And He commanded us to preach to the people, and to testify that it is He who was ordained by God to be Judge of the living and the dead.

✧

ROMANS 2:11

For there is no partiality with God.

✧

ROMANS 5:18

Therefore, as through one man's offense judgment came to all men, resulting in condemnation, even so through one Man's righteous act the free gift came to all men, resulting in justification of life.

✧

ROMANS 5:19

For as by one man's disobedience many were made sinners, so also by one Man's obedience many will be made righteous.

ROMANS 6:23

For the wages of sin is death, but the gift of God is eternal life in Christ Jesus our Lord.

ROMANS 8:26

Likewise the Spirit also helps in our weaknesses. For we do not know what we should pray for as we ought, but the Spirit Himself makes intercession for us with groanings which cannot be uttered.

ROMANS 8:36

As it is written: "For Your sake we are killed all day long; We are accounted as sheep for the slaughter."

I CORINTHIANS 10:13

No temptation has overtaken you except such as is common to man; but God is faithful, who will not allow you to be tempted beyond what you are able, but with the temptation will also make the way of escape, that you may be able to bear it.

I CORINTHIANS 15:43

It is sown in dishonor, it is raised in glory. It is sown in weakness, it is raised in power.

EPHESIANS 4:4

There is one body and one Spirit, just as you were called in one hope of your calling;

EPHESIANS 4:6

one God and Father of all, who is above all, and through all, and in you all.

EPHESIANS 4:7

But to each one of us grace was given according to the measure of Christ's gift.

✧

COLOSSIANS 1:16

For by Him all things were created that are in heaven and that are on earth, visible and invisible, whether thrones or dominions or principalities or powers. All things were created through Him and for Him.

✧

COLOSSIANS 1:17

And He is before all things, and in Him all things consist.

✧

COLOSSIANS 1:21

And you, who once were alienated and enemies in your mind by wicked works, yet now He has reconciled

✧

COLOSSIANS 2:13

And you, being dead in your trespasses and the uncircumcision of your flesh, He has made alive together with Him, having forgiven you all trespasses,

✧

PSALM 47:8

God reigns over the nations; God sits on His holy throne.

✧

PSALM 75:6

For exaltation comes neither from the east Nor from the west nor from the south.

✧

PSALM 75:7

But God is the Judge: He puts down one, And exalts another.

✧

PSALM 111:10

The fear of the Lord is the beginning of wisdom; A good understanding have all those who do His commandments. His praise endures forever.

✧

PSALM 112:1

Praise the Lord! Blessed is the man who fears the LORD, Who delights greatly in His commandments.

PSALM 112:7

He will not be afraid of evil tidings; His heart is steadfast, trusting in the LORD.

PSALM 112:8

His heart is established; He will not be afraid, Until he sees his desire upon his enemies.

PSALM 119:93

I will never forget Your precepts, For by them You have given me life.

PROVERB 8:21

That I may cause those who love me to inherit wealth, That I may fill their treasuries.

PROVERB 10:22

The blessing of the Lord makes one rich, And He adds no sorrow with it.

PROVERB 10:29

The way of the LORD is strength for the upright, But destruction will come to the workers of iniquity.

ISAIAH 48:17

Thus says the LORD, your Redeemer, The Holy One of Israel: "I am the Lord your God, Who teaches you to profit, Who leads you by the way you should go.

ISAIAH 54:17

No weapon formed against you shall prosper, And every tongue which rises against you in judgment You shall condemn.

ISAIAH 65:24

"It shall come to pass that before they call, I will answer; And while they are still speaking, I will hear.

ISAIAH 66:22

"For as the new heaven and the new earth Which I will make shall remain before Me" says the LORD.

MARK 12:27

"He is not the God of the dead, but the God of the living. You are therefore greatly mistaken."

MARK 13:31

"Heaven and earth will pass away, but My words will by no means pass away.

LUKE 1:52

He has put down the mighty from their thrones, And exalted the lowly.

LUKE 11:28

But He said, "More than that, blessed are those who hear the word of God and keep it!"

LUKE 15:10

"Likewise, I say to you, there is joy in the presence of the angels of God over one sinner who repents.

LUKE 16:10

"He who is faithful in what is least is faithless also in much; and he who is unjust in what is least is unjust also in much.

JOHN 3:34

"For He whom God has sent speaks the words of God, for God does not give the Spirit by measure.

JOHN 3:35

"The Father loves the Son, and has given all things into His hand.

JOHN 5:21

"For as the Father raises the dead and gives life to them, even so the Son gives life to whom He will.

JOHN 6:63

"It is the Spirit who gives life; the flesh profits nothing. The words that I speak to you are spirit, and they are life.

JOHN 9:5

"As long as I am in the world, I am the light of the world."

JOHN 10:7

Then Jesus said to them again, "Most assuredly, I say to you, I am the door of the sheep.

JOHN 10:9

"I am the door. If anyone enters by Me, he will be saved, and will go in and out and find pasture.

JOHN 11:25

Jesus said to her, "I am the resurrection and the life. He who believes in Me, though he may die, he shall live.

JOHN 14:13

"And whatever you ask in My name, that I will do, that the Father may be glorified in the Son.

JOHN 14:14

"If you ask anything in My name, I will do it.

JOHN 14:19

"A little while longer and the world will see Me no more, but you will see Me, Because I live, you will live also.

JOHN 14:20

"At that day you will know that I am in My Father, and you in Me and I in you.

JOHN 14:26

"But the Helper, the Holy Spirit, whom the Father will send in My name, He will teach you all things, and bring to you remembrance all things that I said to you.

JOHN 15:11

"These things I have spoken to you, that My joy may remain in you, and that your joy may be full.

ACTS 17:28

"for in Him we live and move and have our being, as also some of your own poets have said, 'For we are also His offspring.'

ACTS 24:15

"I have hope in God, which they themselves also accept, that there will be a resurrection of the dead, both of the just and the unjust.

ACTS 26:23

"that the Christ would suffer, that He would be the first to rise from the dead, and would proclaim light to the Jewish people and to the Gentiles."

ROMANS 1:18

For the wrath of God is revealed from heaven against all ungodliness and unrighteousness of men, who suppress the truth in unrighteousness,

❖

ROMANS 3:20

Therefore by the deeds of the law no flesh will be justified in His sight, for by the law is the knowledge of sin.

❖

ROMANS 3:23

for all have sinned and fall short of the glory of God,

❖

ROMANS 5:1

Therefore, having been justified by faith, we have peace with God through our Lord Jesus Christ,

❖

ROMANS 5:8

But God demonstrates His own love toward us, in that while we were still sinners, Christ died for us.

❖

ROMANS 5:11

And not only that, but we also rejoice in God through our Lord Jesus Christ, through whom we have now received the reconciliation.

❖

ROMANS 6:3

Or do you not know that as many of us as were baptized into Christ Jesus were baptized into His death?

❖

ROMANS 6:4

Therefore we were buried with Him through baptism into death, that just as Christ was raised from the dead by the glory of the Father, even so we also should walk in newness of life.

❖

ROMANS 6:5

For if we have been united together in the likeness of His death, certainly we also shall be in the likeness of His resurrection,

❖

ROMANS 6:6

knowing this, that our old man was crucified with Him, that the body of sin might be done away with, that we should no longer be slaves of sin.

ROMANS 6:9

knowing that Christ, having been raised from the dead, dies no more.
Death no longer has dominion over Him.

ROMANS 6:10

For the death that He died, He died to sin once for all; but the life that He
lives, He lives to God.

ROMANS 14:8

For if we live, we live to the Lord; and if we die, we die to the Lord.
Therefore, whether we live or die, we are the Lord's.

I CORINTHIANS 3:23

And you are Christ's, and Christ is God's.

I CORINTHIANS 8:6

yet for us there is one God, the Father, of whom are all things, and we for
Him; and one Lord Jesus Christ, through whom are all things and through
whom we live.

I CORINTHIANS 10:26

for "the earth is the Lord's, and all its fullness."

II CORINTHIANS 1:21

Now He who establishes us with you in Christ and has anointed us is God,

II CORINTHIANS 1:22

who also has sealed us and given us the Spirit in our hearts as a guarantee.

II CORINTHIANS 2:14

Now thanks be to God who always leads us in triumph in Christ, and
through us diffuses the fragrance of His knowledge in every place.

II CORINTHIANS 4:14

knowing that He who raised up the Lord Jesus will also raise us up with Jesus, and will present us with you.

II CORINTHIANS 5:7

For we walk by faith, not by sight.

II CORINTHIANS 5:8

We are confident, yes, well pleased, rather to be absent from the body and to be present with the Lord.

GALATIANS 3:28

There is neither Jew nor Greek, there is neither slave nor free, there is neither male nor female; for you are all one in Christ Jesus.

GALATIANS 5:24

And those who are in Christ's have crucified the flesh with its passion and desires.

EPHESIANS 1:7

In Him we have redemption through His blood, the forgiveness of sins, according to the riches of His grace

EPHESIANS 1:11

In Him also we have obtained an inheritance, being predestined according to the purpose of Him who works all things according to the counsel of His will,

EPHESIANS 2:14

For He Himself is our peace, who has made both one, and has broken down the middle wall of separation,

EPHESIANS 2:20

having been built on the foundation of the apostles and prophets, Jesus Christ Himself being the chief cornerstone,

EPHESIANS 3:2

if indeed you have heard of the dispensation of the grace of God which was given to me for you,

✧

EPHESIANS 3:6

that the Gentiles should be fellow heirs, of the same body, and partakers of His promise in Christ through the gospel,

✧

EPHESIANS 3:19

to know the love of Christ which passes knowledge; that you may be filled with all the fullness of God.

✧

EPHESIANS 5:20

giving thanks always for all things to God the Father in the name of our Lord Jesus Christ,

✧

HEBREWS 6:13

For when God made a promise to Abraham, because He could swear by no one greater, He swore by Himself,

✧

HEBREWS 6:14

saying, "Surely blessing I will bless you, and multiplying I will multiply you."

✧

HEBREWS 6:17

Thus God, determining to show more abundantly to the heirs of promise the immutability of His counsel, confirmed it by an oath,

✧

HEBREWS 6:18

that by two immutable things, in which it is impossible for God to lie, we might have strong consolation, who have fled for refuge to lay hold of the hope set before us.

✧

HEBREWS 7:22
by so much more Jesus has become a surety of a better covenant.

✧

HEBREWS 7:24
But He, because He continues forever, has an unchangeable priesthood.

✧

HEBREWS 7:25
Therefore He is also able to save to the uttermost those who come to God through Him, since He always lives to make intercession for them.

✧

HEBREWS 9:11
But Christ came as High Priest of the good things to come, with the greater and more perfect tabernacle not made with hands, that is, not of this creation.

✧

HEBREWS 9:14
how much more shall the blood of Christ, who through the eternal Spirit offered Himself without spot to God, cleanse your conscience from dead works to serve the living God?

✧

HEBREWS 9:15
And for this reason He is the Mediator of the new covenant, by means of death, for the redemption of the transgressions under the first covenant, that those who are called may receive the promise of the eternal inheritance.

✧

HEBREWS 9:16
For where there is a testament, there must also of necessity be the death of the testator.

✧

HEBREWS 9:17
For a testament is in force after men are dead, since it has no power at all while the testator lives.

✧

HEBREWS 9:22

And according to the law almost all things are purified with blood, and without shedding of blood there is no remission.

HEBREWS 9:27

And as it is appointed for men to die once, but after this the judgment,

HEBREWS 9:28

so Christ was offered once to bear the sins of many. To those who eagerly wait for Him He will appear a second time, apart from sin, for salvation.

HEBREWS 10:16

"This is the covenant that I will make with them after those days, says the LORD: I will put My laws into their hearts, and in their minds I will write them,"

HEBREWS 10:17

then He adds, "Their sins and their lawless deeds I will remember no more."

HEBREWS 10:31

It is a fearful thing to fall into the hands of the living God.

III JOHN 1:4

I have no greater joy than to hear that my children walk in truth.

II CHRONICLES 16:9

"For the eyes of the LORD run to and fro throughout the whole earth to show Himself strong on behalf of those whose heart is loyal to Him.

JEREMIAH 10:10

But the Lord is the true God; He is the living God the everlasting king. At His wrath the earth will tremble, And the nations will not be able to endure His indignation.

◇

JEREMIAH 17:10

I, the LORD, search the heart, I test the mind, Even to give every man according to His ways, According to the fruit of his doings.

◇

JEREMIAH 32:27

"Behold, I am the Lord, the God of all flesh. Is there anything too hard for Me?

◇

JEREMIAH 33:2

"Thus says the LORD who made it, the LORD who formed it to establish it (the LORD is His name):

◇

EZEKIEL 18:4

"Behold, all souls are Mine; The soul of the father As well as the soul of the son is Mine; The soul who sins shall die.

◇

DANIEL 6:26

I make a decree that in ever dominion of my kingdom men must tremble and fear before the God of Daniel. For He is the living God, And steadfast forever; His kingdom is the one which shall not be destroyed, And His dominion shall endure to the end.

◇

HOSEA 4:6

My people are destroyed for lack of knowledge. Because you have rejected knowledge, I also will reject you from being priest for Me; Because you have forgotten the law of your God, I also will forget your children.

◇

HOSEA 6:6

For I desire mercy and not sacrifice, And the knowledge of God more than burnt offerings.

◇

HOSEA 10:12

Sow for yourselves righteousness; Reap in mercy; Break up your fallow ground, For it is time to seek the LORD, Till He comes and rains righteousness on you.

HAGGAI 2:8
'The silver in Mine, and the gold is Mine, says the Lord of hosts.

✧

MATTHEW 10:22
"And you will be hated by all for My name's sake. But he who endures to the end will be saved.

✧

MATTHEW 12:31
"Therefore I say to you, every sin and blasphemy will be forgiven men, but the blasphemy against the Spirit will not be forgiven men.

✧

MATTHEW 12:32
"Anyone who speaks a word against the Son of Man, it will be forgiven him; but whoever speaks against the Holy Spirit, it will not be forgiven him, either in this age or in the age to come.

✧

MATTHEW 12:36
"But I say to you that for every idle word men may speak, they will give account of it in the day of judgment.

✧

MATTHEW 12:37
"For by your words you will be justified, and by your words you will be condemned. "

✧

MATTHEW 12:40
"For as Jonah was three days and three nights in the belly of the great fish, so will the Son of Man be three days and three nights in the heart of the earth.

✧

MATTHEW 16:19
"And I will give you the keys of the kingdom of heaven, and whatever you bind on earth will be bound in heaven, and whatever you loose on earth will be loosed in heaven."

✧

MARK 11:24

"Therefore I say to you, whatever things you ask when you pray, believe that you receive them, and you will have them.

⟡

MARK 11:25

"And whenever you stand praying, if you have anything against anyone, forgive him, that your Father in heaven may also forgive you your trespasses.

⟡

MARK 14:38

"Watch and pray, lest you enter into temptation. The spirit indeed is willing, but the flesh is weak."

⟡

LUKE 5:32

"I have not come to call the righteous, but sinners, to repentance."

⟡

LUKE 12:23

"Life is more than food, and the body is more than clothing.

⟡

LUKE 12:34

"For where you treasure is, there your heart will be also.

⟡

LUKE 17:21

"nor will they say, 'See here!' or 'See there!' For indeed, the kingdom of God is within you."

⟡

LUKE 21:33

"Heaven and earth will pass away, but My words will by no means pass away.

⟡

JOHN 3:3

Jesus answered and said to him, "Most assuredly, I say to you, unless one is born again, he cannot see the kingdom of God."

⟡

JOHN 3:5

Jesus answered, "Most assuredly, I say to you, unless one is born of water and the spirit, he cannot enter the kingdom of God.

✧

JOHN 3:15

"that whoever believes in Him should not perish but have eternal life.

✧

JOHN 4:24

"God is Spirit, and those who worship Him must worship in Spirit and truth."

✧

JOHN 5:22

"For the Father judges no one, but has committed all judgment to the Son,

✧

JOHN 5:23

"that all should honor the Son, just as they honor the Father. He who does not honor the Son does not honor the Father who sent Him.

✧

JOHN 5:27

"and has given Him authority to execute judgment also, because He is the Son of Man.

✧

JOHN 6:58

"This is the bread which came down form heaven-not as your fathers ate the manna, and are dead. He who eats this bread will live forever."

✧

JOHN 7:24

"Do not judge according to appearance, but judge with righteous judgment."

✧

JOHN 7:38

"He who believes in Me, as the Scripture has said, out of his heart will flow rivers of living water."

✧

JOHN 8:32

"And you shall know the truth, and the truth shall make you free."

✧

JOHN 8:36

"Therefore if the Son makes you free, you shall be free indeed.

✧

JOHN 12:46

"I have come as a light into the world, that whoever believes in Me should not abide in darkness.

✧

JOHN 12:49

"For I have not spoken on My own authority; but the Father who sent Me gave Me a command, what I should say and what I should speak.

✧

JOHN 12:50

"And I know that His command is everlasting life. Therefore, whatever I speak, just as the Father has told Me, so I speak."

✧

JOHN 13:34

"A new commandment I give to you, that you love one another; as I have loved you, that you also love one another.

✧

JOHN 14:23

Jesus answered and said to him, "If anyone loves Me, he will keep My word; and My Father will love him, and We will come to him and make Our home with him.

✧

JOHN 14:24

"He who does not love Me does not keep My words; and the word which you hear is not Mine but the Father's who sent Me.

✧

JOHN 15:7

"If you abide in Me, and My words abide in you, you will ask what you desire, and it shall be done for you.

✧

✧

JOHN 15:9

"As the Father loved Me, I also have loved you; abide in My love.

✧

JOHN 16:7

"Nevertheless I tell you the truth. It is to your advantage that I go away; for if I do not go away; the Helper will not come to you; but if I depart, I will send Him to you.

✧

JOHN 16:23

"And in that day you will ask Me nothing. Most assuredly, I say to you, whatever you ask the Father in My name He will give you.

✧

JOHN 16:33

"These things I have spoken to you, that in Me you may have peace. In the world you will have tribulation; but be of good cheer, I have overcome the world."

✧

JOHN 17:3

"And this is eternal life, that they may know You, the only true God, and Jesus Christ whom You have sent.

✧

JOHN 21:23

Then this saying went out among the brethren that this disciple would not die. Yet Jesus did not say to him that he would not die, but, "If I will that he remain till I come, what is that to you?"

✧

ACTS 4:12

"Nor is there salvation in any other, for there is no other name under heaven given among men by which we must be saved."

✧

ACTS 10:43

"To Him all the prophets witness that, through His name, whoever believes in Him will receive remission of sins."

✧

ROMANS 6:5

For if we have been united together in the likeness of His death, certainly we also shall be in the likeness of His resurrection,

ROMANS 6:6

knowing this, that our old man was crucified with Him, that the body of sin might be done away with, that we should no longer be slaves of sin.

ROMANS 6:11

Likewise you also, reckon yourselves to be dead indeed to sin, but alive to God in Christ Jesus our Lord.

ROMANS 10:1

Brethren, my heart's desire and prayer to God for Israel is that they may be saved.

ROMANS 12:2

And do not be conformed to this world, but be transformed, by the renewing of your mind, that you may prove what is that good and acceptable and perfect will of God.

ROMANS 13:2

Therefore whoever resists the authority resists the ordinance of God, and those who resist will bring judgment on themselves.

ROMANS 14:8

For if we live, we live to the Lord; and if we die, we die to the Lord. Therefore, whether we live or die, we are the Lord's.

ROMANS 14:11

For it is written: "As I live, says the Lord, Every knee shall bow to Me, And every tongue shall confess to God."

ROMANS 14:12

So then each of us shall give account of Himself to God.

I CORINTHIANS 2:5

that your faith should not be in the wisdom of men but in the power of God.

I CORINTHIANS 3:16

Do you not know that you are the temple of God and that the Spirit of God dwells in you?

I CORINTHIANS 3:17

If anyone defiles the temple of God, God will destroy him. For the temple of God is holy, which temple you are.

I CORINTHIANS 6:19

Or do you not know that your body is the temple of the Holy Spirit who is in you, whom you have from God, and you are not your own?

I CORINTHIANS 6:20

For you were bought at a price; therefore glorify God in your body and in your spirit, which are God's.

I THESSALONIANS 4:7

For God did not call us to uncleanness, but in holiness.

I THESSALONIANS 4:9

But concerning brotherly love you have no need that I should write to you, for you yourselves are taught by God to love one another;

I THESSALONIANS 4:11

that you also aspire to lead a quiet life, to mind your own business, and to work with your own hands, as we commanded you,

I THESSALONIANS 5:15

See that no one renders evil for evil to anyone, but always pursue what is good both for yourselves and for all.

HEBREWS 12:29

For our God is a consuming fire.

HEBREWS 13:5

Let your conduct be without covetousness; be content with such things as you have. For He Himself has said, "I will never leave you nor forsake you."

II PETER 1:3

as His divine power has given to us all things that pertain to life and godliness through the knowledge of Him who called us by glory and virtue,

II PETER 3:8

But, beloved, do not forget this one thing, that with the Lord one day is as a thousand years, and a thousand years as one day.

JOB 5:6

For affliction does not come from the dust, Nor does trouble spring from the ground;

JOB 5:7

Yet man is born to trouble, As the sparks fly upward.

JOB 8:22

Those who hate you will be clothed with shame, And the dwelling place of the wicked will come to nothing."

JOB 12:10

In whose hand is the life of every living thing, And the breath of all mankind?

JOB 12:12

Wisdom is with aged men, And with length of days, understanding.

JOB 12:13

"With Him are wisdom and strength, He has counsel and understanding.

JOB 28:28

And to man He said, 'Behold, the fear of the Lord, that is wisdom, And to depart from evil is understanding.'"

JOB 36:4

For truly my words are not false; One who is perfect in knowledge is with you.

JOB 36:5

'Behold, God is mighty, but despises no one; He is mighty in strength of understanding.

JOB 36:6

He does not preserve the life of the wicked, But gives justice to the oppressed.

JOB 36:7

He does not withdraw His eyes from the righteous; But they are on the throne with kings, For He has seated them forever, And they are exalted.

PSALM 3:8

Salvation belongs to the Lord. Your blessing is upon Your people.

PSALM 77:14

You are the God who does wonders; You have declared Your strength among the peoples.

PROVERB 8:13

The fear of the Lord is to hate evil; Pride and arrogance and the evil way And the perverse mouth I hate.

JEREMIAH 31:1

"At the same time," says the Lord, "I will be the God of all the families of Israel, and they shall be My people."

·✧·

DANIEL 2:28

"But there is a God in heaven who reveals secrets, and He has made known to King Ne•bú•chadnez'zar what will be in the latter days. Your dream, and the visions of your head upon your bed, were these:

·✧·

NAHUM 1:2

God is jealous, and the Lord avenges; The Lord avenges and is furious. The Lord will take vengeance on His adversaries, And He reserves wrath for His enemies;

·✧·

MATTHEW 6:24

"No one can serve two masters; for either he will hate the one, and love the other, or else he will be loyal to the one and despise the other. You cannot serve God and mammon.

·✧·

MATTHEW 12:50

"For whoever does the will of My Father in heaven is My brother and sister and mother."

·✧·

JOHN 12:32

"And I, if I am lifted up from the earth, will draw all peoples to Myself."

·✧·

ROMANS 3:4

Certainly not! Indeed, let God be true but every man a liar. As it is written: " That You may be justified in Your words, And may overcome when You are judged."

·✧·

ROMANS 8:1

There is therefore now no condemnation to those who are in Christ Jesus, who do not walk according to the flesh, but according to the Spirit.

·✧·

ROMANS 8:13

For if you live according to the flesh you will die; but if by the Spirit you put to death the deeds of the body, you will live.

·✧·

✧

ROMANS 8:27

Now He who searches the hearts knows what the mind of the Spirit is, because He makes intercession for the saints according to the will of God.

✧

ROMANS 8:28

And we know that all things work together for good to those who love God, to those who are the called according to His purpose.

✧

I CORINTHIANS 6:14

And God both raised up the Lord and will also raise us up by His power.

✧

I CORINTHIANS 15:44

It is sown a natural body, it is raised a spiritual body. There is a natural body, and there is a spiritual body.

✧

II CORINTHIANS 1:3

Blessed be the God and Father of our Lord Jesus Christ, the Father of mercies and God of all comfort,

✧

II CORINTHIANS 5:15

and He died for all, that those who live should live no longer for themselves, but for Him who died for them and rose again.

✧

GALATIANS 3:6

just as Abraham "believed God, and it was accounted to him for righteousness."

✧

GALATIANS 3:8

And the Scripture, foreseeing that God would justify the Gentiles by faith, preached the gospel to Abraham beforehand, saying, "In you all the nations shall be blessed."

✧

GALATIANS 3:14

that the blessings of Abraham might come upon the Gentile in Christ Jesus, that we might receive the promise of the Spirit through faith.

GALATIANS 3:26
For you are all sons of God through faith in Christ Jesus.

⟡

GALATIANS 3:27
For as many of you as were baptized into Christ have put on Christ.

⟡

EPHESIANS 2:14
For He Himself is our peace, who has made both one, and has broken down the middle wall of separation,

⟡

EPHESIANS 3:6
that the Gentiles should be fellow heirs, of the same body, and partakes of His promise in Christ through the gospel,

⟡

PHILIPPIANS 1:6
being confident of this very thing, that He who has begun a good work in you will complete it until the day of Jesus Christ;

⟡

PSALM 29:3
The voice of the Lord is over the waters; The God of glory thunders; the Lord is over many waters.

⟡

PSALM 29:4
The voice of the Lord is powerful; The voice of the Lord is full of majesty.

⟡

PSALM 118:17
I shall not die, but live, And declare the works of the Lord.

⟡

PSALM 119:89
Forever, O Lord, Your word is settled in heaven.

⟡

PSALM 121:4
Behold, He who keeps, Israel Shall neither slumber nor sleep.

⟡

⟡

PSALM 135:5

For I know that the Lord is great, And our Lord is above all gods.

⟡

PSALM 135:6

Whatever the Lord pleases He does, In heaven and in earth, In the seas and in all deep places.

⟡

PSALM 145:20

The Lord preserves all who love Him, But all the wicked He will destroy.

⟡

PROVERB 1:7

The fear of the Lord is the beginning of knowledge, But fools despise wisdom and instruction.

⟡

PROVERB 10:31

The mouth of the righteous brings forth wisdom, But the perverse tongue will be cut out.

⟡

PROVERB 10:32

The lips of the righteous know what is acceptable, But the mouth of the wicked what is perverse.

⟡

PROVERB 11:17

The merciful man does good for his own soul, But he who is cruel troubles his own flesh.

⟡

PROVERB 14:27

The fear of the Lord is a fountain of life, To turn one away from the snares of death.

⟡

PROVERB 15:3

The eyes of the Lord are in every place, Keeping watch on the evil and the good.

⟡

PROVERB 16:7

When a man's ways please the Lord, He makes even his enemies to be at peace with him.

✧

PROVERB 16:17

The highway of the upright is to depart from evil; He who keeps his way preserves his soul.

✧

PROVERB 18:21

Death and life are in the power of the tongue, And those who love it will eat its fruit.

✧

PROVERB 19:5

A false witness will not go unpunished, And he who speaks lies will not escape.

✧

PROVERB 19:23

The fear of the Lord leads to life, And he who has it will abide in satisfaction; He will not be visited with evil.

✧

PROVERB 20:27

The spirit of a man is the lamp of the Lord, Searching all the inner depths of his heart.

✧

PROVERB 21:3

To do righteousness and justice Is more acceptable to the Lord than sacrifice.

✧

PROVERB 21:21

He who follows righteousness and mercy Finds life, righteousness and honor.

✧

PROVERB 21:23

Whoever guards his mouth and tongue Keeps his soul from troubles.

✧

✧

PROVERB 30:5

Every word of God is pure; He is a shield to those who put their
trust in Him.

✧

ECCLESIASTES 3:14

I know that whatever God does, It shall be forever. Nothing can be added
to it, And nothing taken from it. God does it, that men should
fear before Him.

✧

ECCLESIASTES 3:15

That which is has already been, And what is to be has already been; And
God requires an account of what is past.

✧

ISAIAH 33:22

(For the LORD is our Judge, The Lord is our Lawgiver, The Lord is our
King; He will save us);

✧

ISAIAH 42:8

I am the LORD, that is My name; And My glory I will not give to another,
Nor My praise to carved images.

✧

ISAIAH 43:11

I, even I, am the LORD, And besides Me there is no savior.

✧

ISAIAH 43:15

I am the LORD, your Holy One, The Creator of Israel, your King."

✧

ISAIAH 43:25

I, even I, am He who blots out your transgressions for My own sake; And I
will not remember your sins.

✧

ISAIAH 45:15

Truly You are God, who hide Yourself, O God of
Israel, the Savior!

✧

ISAIAH 49:26

I will feed those who oppress you with their own flesh, And they shall be drunk with their own blood as with sweet wine. All flesh shall know That I, the Lord, am your Savior, And your Redeemer, the Mighty One of Jacob."

⟡

ISAIAH 55:11

So shall My word be that goes forth from My mouth; It shall not return to Me void, But it shall accomplish what I please, And it shall prosper in the thing for which I sent it.

⟡

ISAIAH 66:1

Thus says the LORD: "Heaven is My throne, And earth is My footstool. Where is the house that you will build Me? And where is the place of My rest?

⟡

ISAIAH 66:15

For behold, the Lord will come with fire And with His chariots, like a whirlwind, To render His anger with fury, And His rebuke with flames of fire.

⟡

JEREMIAH 17:5

Thus says the LORD: "Cursed is the man who trusts in man And makes flesh his strength, Whose heart departs from the Lord.

⟡

JEREMIAH 23:23

"Am I a God near at hand," says the LORD, "And not a God afar off?

⟡

JEREMIAH 23:24

Can anyone hide himself in secret places, So I shall not see him?" says the LORD; "Do I not fill heaven and earth?" says the Lord.

⟡

JEREMIAH 23:29

"Is not My word like a fire?" says the LORD, "And like a hammer that breaks the rock in pieces?

⟡

JEREMIAH 51:15

He has made the earth by His power; He has established the world by His wisdom, And stretched out the heaven by His understanding.

✧

EZEKIEL 33:11

"Say to them: 'As I live,' says the Lord GOD, 'I have no pleasure in the death of the wicked, but that the wicked turn from his way and live. Turn, turn from your evil ways! For why should you die, O house of Israel?'

✧

DANIEL 2:21

And He changes the times and the seasons; He removes kings and raises up kings; He gives wisdom to the wise And knowledge to those who have understanding.

✧

DANIEL 2:22

He reveals deep and secret things; He knows what is in the darkness And light dwells with Him.

✧

AMOS 3:3

Can two walk together, unless they are agreed?

✧

ZECHARIAH 2:5

'For I,' say the LORD, 'will be a wall of fire all around her, and I will be the glory in her midst.'"

✧

ZECHARIAH 2:11

"Many nations shall be joined to the LORD in that day, and they shall become My people. And I will dwell in your midst. Then you will know that the LORD of hosts has sent Me to you.

✧

ZECHARIAH 14:1

Behold, the day of the LORD is coming, And your spoil will be divided in your midst.

✧

MATTHEW 7:14
"Because narrow is the gate and difficult is the way which leads to life, and there are few who find it.

MATTHEW 10:36
"and 'a man's enemies will be those of his own household.'

MATTHEW 18:20
"For where two or three are gathered together in My name, I am there in the midst of them."

MATTHEW 24:14
"And this gospel of the kingdom will be preached in all the world as a witness to all the nations, and then the end will come.

MARK 12:25
"For when they rise from the dead, they neither marry nor are given in marriage, but are like angels in heaven.

LUKE 8:17
"For nothing is secret that will not be revealed, nor anything hidden that will not be known and come to light.

LUKE 11:17
But He, knowing their thoughts, said to them: "Every kingdom divided against itself is brought to desolation, and a house divided against a house falls.

LUKE 11:34
"The lamp of the body is the eye. Therefore, when your eye is good, your whole body also is full of light. But when your eye is bad, your body also is full of darkness.

LUKE 12:23
"Life is more than food, and the body is more than clothing.

LUKE 12:34

✧

"For where your treasure is, there your heart will be also.

✧

LUKE 24:7

"saying, 'The Son of Man must be delivered into the hands of sinful men, and be crucified, and the third day rise again.'"

✧

LUKE 24:44

Then He said to them, "These are the words which I spoke to you while I was still with you, that all things must be fulfilled which were written in the Law of Moses and the Prophets, and the Psalms concerning me."

✧

LUKE 24:46

Then He said to them, "Thus it is written, and thus it was necessary for the Christ to suffer and to rise from the dead the third day,

✧

JOHN 1:3

All things were made through Him, and without Him nothing was made that was made.

✧

JOHN 1:10

He was in the world, and the world was made through Him, and the world did not know Him.

✧

JOHN 1:11

He came to His own, and His own did not receive Him.

✧

JOHN 1:13

who were born, not of blood, nor of the will of the flesh, nor of the will of man, but of God.

✧

JOHN 1:17

For the law was given through Moses, but grace and truth came through Jesus Christ.

✧

⟡

JOHN 3:31

"He who comes from above is above all; he who is of the earth is earthly and speaks of the earth. He who comes from heaven is above all.

⟡

JOHN 5:25

"Most assuredly, I say to you, the hour is coming, and now is, when the dead will hear the voice of the Son of God; and those who hear will live.

⟡

JOHN 5:26

"For as the Father has life in Himself, so He has granted the Son to have life in Himself,

⟡

JOHN 8:16

"And yet if I do judge, My judgment is true; for I am not alone, but I am with the Father who sent Me.

⟡

JOHN 8:18

"I am One who bears witness of Myself, and the Father who sent Me bears witness of Me."

⟡

JOHN 8:23

And He said to them, "You are from beneath; I am from above. You are of this world; I am not of this world.

⟡

JOHN 8:45

"But because I tell the truth, you do not believe Me.

⟡

JOHN 11:25

Jesus said to her, "I am the resurrection and the life. He who believes in Me, though he may die, he shall live.

⟡

JOHN 11:40

Jesus said to her, "Did I not say to you that if you would believe you would see the glory of God?"

⟡

✧

JOHN 12:48

"He who rejects Me, and does not receive My words, has that which judges him- the word that I have spoken will judge him in the last day.

✧

JOHN 14:10

"Do you not believe that I am in the Father, and the Father in Me? The words that I speak to you I do not speak on My own authority; but the Father who dwells in Me does the works.

✧

JOHN 14:11

"Believe Me that I am in the Father and the Father in Me, or else believe Me for the sake of the works themselves.

✧

JOHN 15:1

"I am the true vine, and My Father is the vinedresser.

✧

JOHN 15:8

"By this My Father is glorified, that you bear much fruit; so you will be My disciples.

✧

JOHN 15:26

"But when the Helper comes, whom I shall send to you from the Father, the Spirit of truth who proceeds from the Father, He will testify of Me.

✧

JOHN 16:14

"He will glorify Me, for He will take of what is Mine and declare it to you.

✧

JOHN 16:28

"I came forth from the Father and have come into the world. Again, I leave the world and go to the Father."

✧

JOHN 17:2

"as You have given Him authority over all flesh, that He should give eternal life to as many as You have given Him.

✧

JOHN 17:16

"They are not of the world, just as I am not of the world.

ACTS 3:23

'And it shall be that every soul who will not hear that Prophet shall be utterly destroyed from among the people.'

I CORINTHIANS 4:20

For the kingdom of God is not in word but in power.

I CORINTHIANS 6:9

Do you not know that the unrighteous will not inherit the kingdom of God? Do not be deceived. Neither fornicators, nor idolaters, nor adulterers, nor homosexuals, nor sodomites.

I CORINTHIANS 6:10

nor thieves, nor covetous, nor drunkards, nor revilers, nor extortioners will inherit the kingdom of God.

I CORINTHIANS 15:26

The last enemy that will be destroyed is death.

I CORINTHIANS 15:45

And so it is written, "The first man Adam became a living being" The last Adam became a lifegiving spirit.

I CORINTHIANS 15:51

Behold, I tell you a mystery: We shall not all sleep, but we shall all be changed-

II CORINTHIANS 4:18

While we do not look at the things which are seen, but at the things which are seen. For the things which are seen are temporary, but the things which are not seen are eternal.

✧

II CORINTHIANS 5:7
For we walk by faith, not by sight.

✧

II CORINTHIANS 5:10
For we must all appear before the judgment seat of Christ, that each one may receive the things done in the body, according to what he has done, whether good or bad.

✧

II CORINTHIANS 5:17
Therefore, if anyone is in Christ, he is a new creation; old things have passed away; behold all things have become new.

✧

II CORINTHIANS 9:6
But this I say: He who sows sparingly will also reap sparingly, and he who sows bountifully will also reap bountifully.

✧

II CORINTHIANS 10:3
For though we walk in the flesh, we do not war according to the flesh.

✧

II CORINTHIANS 12:9
And He said to me, "My grace is sufficient for you, for My strength is made perfect in weakness" Therefore most gladly I will rather boast in my infirmities, that the power of Christ may rest upon me.

✧

GALATIANS 3:28
There is neither Jew nor Greek, there is neither slave nor free, there is neither male nor female; for you are all one in Christ Jesus.

✧

EPHESIANS 6:12
For we do not wrestle against flesh and blood, but against principalities, against powers, against the rulers of the darkness of this age, against spiritual hosts of wickedness in the heavenly places.

✧

II TIMOTHY 3:12
Yes, and all who desire to live godly in Christ Jesus will suffer persecution.

✧

II TIMOTHY 4:1

I charge you therefore before God and the Lord Jesus Christ, who will judge the living and the dead at His appearing and His kingdom:

✧

TITUS 1:15

To the pure all things are pure, but to those who are defiled and unbelieving nothing is pure; but even their mind and conscience are defiled.

✧

HEBREWS 9:16

For where there is a testament, there must also of necessity be the death of the testator.

✧

HEBREWS 9:17

For a testament is in force after men are dead, since it has no power at all while the testator lives.

✧

HEBREWS 9:22

And according to the law almost all things are purified with blood, and without shedding of blood there is no remission.

✧

HEBREWS 9:27

And as it is appointed for men to die once, but after this the judgment.

✧

HEBREWS 9:28

so Christ was offered once to bear the sins of many. To those who eagerly wait for Him He will appear a second time, apart from sin, for salvation.

✧

HEBREWS 10:16

"This is the covenant that I will make with them after those days, says the Lord: I will put My laws into their hearts, and in their minds I will write them,"

✧

HEBREWS 10:30

For we know Him who said, "Vengeance is Mine, I will repay," says the Lord. And again, "The Lord will judge His people."

◇

HEBREWS 10:38

Now the just shall live by faith; But if anyone draws back, My soul has no pleasure in him."

◇

HEBREWS 12:2

Looking unto Jesus, the author and finisher of our faith, who for the joy that was set before Him endured the cross despising the shame, and has sat down at the right hand of the throne of God.

◇

JAMES 2:26

For as the body without the spirit is dead, so faith without works is dead also.

◇

II PETER 1:21

for prophecy never came by the will of man, but holy men of God spoke as they were moved by the Holy Spirit.

◇

II PETER 3:13

Nevertheless we, according to His promise, look for new heaven and a new earth in which righteousness dwells.

◇

I JOHN 1:3

that which we have seen and heard we declare to you, that you also may have fellowship with us; and truly our fellowship is with the Father and with His Son Jesus Christ.

◇

I JOHN 1:4

And these things we write to you that your joy may be full.

◇

✧

I JOHN 1:5
This is the message which we have heard from Him and declare to you, that God is light and in Him is no darkness at all.

✧

I JOHN 1:7
But if we walk in the light as He is in the light, we have fellowship with one another, and the blood of Jesus Christ His Son cleanses us from all sin.

✧

I JOHN 2:2
And He Himself is the propitiation for our sins, and not for ours only but also for the whole world.

✧

I JOHN 2:5
But whoever keeps His word, truly the love of God is perfected in him. By this we know that we are in Him.

✧

I JOHN 2:23
Whoever denies the Son does not have the Father either; he who acknowl-edge the Son has the Father also.

✧

I JOHN 2:24
Therefore let that abide in you which you heard from the beginning. If what you heard from the beginning abides in you, you also will abide in the Son and in the Father.

✧

I JOHN 2:29
If you know that He is righteous, you know that everyone who practices righteousness is born of Him.

✧

I JOHN 3:3
And everyone who has this hope in Him purifies himself, just as He is pure.

✧

I JOHN 3:5

And you know that He was manifested to take away our sins, and in Him there is no sin.

✧

I JOHN 4:4

You are of God, little children, and have overcome them, because He who is in you is greater than he who is in the world.

✧

I JOHN 4:13

By this we know that we abide in Him, and He in us, because He has given us of His Spirit.

✧

I JOHN 4:16

And we have known and believed the love that God has for us. God is love, and he who abides in love abides in God, and God in him.

✧

REVELATION 1:18

"I am He who lives, and was dead, and behold, I am alive forevermore. Amen, And I have the keys of Ha, des and of Death.

✧

I JOHN 4:18

There is no fear in love; but perfect love casts out fear, because fear involves torment. But he who fears has not been made perfect in love.

✧

I JOHN 5:11

And this is the testimony: that God has given us eternal life, and this life is in His Son.

✧

I JOHN 5:12

He who has the Son has life; he who does not have the Son of God does not have life.

✧

✧

I JOHN 5:20

And we know that the Son of God has come and has given us an understanding, that we may know Him who is true; and we are in Him who is true, in His Son Jesus Christ. This is the true God and eternal life.

✧

REVELATION 1:7

Behold, He is coming with clouds, and every eye will see Him, even they who pierced Him. And all the tribes of the earth will mourn because of Him. Even so, Amen.

✧

REVELATION 1:8

"I am the Alpha and the Omega, the Beginning and the End," says the Lord "who is and who was and who is to come, the Almighty."

✧

Salvation

✧

Jesus, I believe you are the Son of God and that you died to save me from my sin and that God raised you from the dead. Jesus forgive me for all of my sins come into my heart and be my Savior and my Lord. I thank you that I am now saved and that I am a child of God. Amen.

Holy Spirit

✧

Heavenly Father, I thank you that Jesus is my Savior and my Lord. I thank you that your word says it I ask for the Holy Spirit, you will give Him to me. I now ask for the Holy Spirit and by faith I believe I received Him. I am now filled with the Holy Spirit and I will speak in other tongues as the Spirit gives me utterance. In Jesus name I thank you. Amen.